SCIENCE AND HERMENEUTICS

Foundations of Contemporary Interpretation
Moisés Silva, Series Editor
Volume 6

SCIENCE AND HERMENEUTICS

Implications of Scientific Method for Biblical Interpretation

Vern Sheridan Poythress

Academie
Books Grand Rapids,
Michigan
Zondervan Publishing House

SCIENCE AND HERMENEUTICS
Copyright © 1988 by Vern S. Poythress

Academie Books is an imprint of Zondervan Publishing House,
1415 Lake Drive, S.E., Grand Rapids, Michigan 49506.

Library of Congress Cataloging in Publication Data

Poythress, Vern S.
    Science and hermeneutics : implications of scientific method for
  Biblical interpretation / Vern Sheridan Poythress.
        p.   cm. — (Foundations of contemporary interpretation : vol. 6)
    Includes bibliographical references.
    ISBN 0-310-40971-3
    1. Bible—Hermeneutics.   2. Bible and science.   Science—
  Methodology.   I. Title.   II. Title: Implications of scientific
  method for Biblical interpretation.   III. Series: Foundations of
  contemporary interpretation ; v. 6.
  BS476.P69 1988
  220.6'01–dc19   88-6216
                                                                     CIP

Edited by Craig Noll
Designed by Louise Bauer

Printed in the United States of America

88   89   90   91   92   93 / CH / 10   9   8   7   6   5   4   3   2   1

To my wife Diane

CONTENTS

EDITOR'S PREFACE

Many years ago, upon reading Thomas S. Kuhn's work *The Structure of Scientific Revolutions*, I was taken aback by the obvious parallels between the subject of that book and the field of biblical exegesis. It seemed strange then—and more so now after all these years—that no one had sought to draw out the implications of Kuhn's ideas for better understanding the conflicts that frequently arise over the interpretation of Scripture.

It would be difficult to find someone better suited to tackle this issue than Vern Poythress. After earning a Ph.D. in mathematics at Harvard University, Poythress developed concurrent interests in the fields of linguistics and theology. Though he later specialized in New Testament studies, receiving a Th.D. in Pauline theology from the University of Stellenbosch, he has continued to pursue his interests in the relationship between science and theology. Indeed, this concern plays a significant role in his teaching of doctoral-level courses in biblical hermeneutics at Westminster Theological Seminary.

The author does not assume any prior knowledge of the field on the part of the reader, but novices and experts alike will surely be fascinated by the clear and perceptive account to be found in this work. A thoughtful reading of Poythress's analysis will help students of the Bible appreciate the origin and nature of interpretive disputes. It will also aid them in developing their own exegetical skills without too quickly dismissing the views of those with whom they disagree.

Moisés Silva

1

HOW SHOULD WE INTERPRET THE BIBLE?

Science has proved remarkably successful as a technique for enhancing our knowledge of the natural world. Can we also learn something from science about how to enhance our knowledge of the Bible?

SHOULD BIBLICAL INTERPRETATION BECOME SCIENTIFIC?

One way of following science is to try to make our study of the Bible "scientific." Would such an approach mean simply that we study the Bible more intensively, more painstakingly? Would it mean that we supply ourselves with all the aids and all the information about the Bible that we can gather? Such steps are obviously useful. They are what we might do with respect to any subject about which we were intensely interested. But such steps by themselves would make us scientific only in a very loose sense. What else might we do? Should we study the Bible "objectively," without ever asking how it affects our own lives personally? But such study would disastrously ignore the Bible's concern to be a means for our spiritual communion with God. If the Bible is God's Word, can it ever be subject to scientific investigation in quite the same way as we would investigate an animal or a plant?

These questions are obviously important, but we cannot explore them all. Questions about whether theology should be scientific will be covered in more detail in another volume in this series on hermeneutics. In this volume, we will explore whether the growth of knowledge in science can tell us something about how knowledge grows in biblical interpretation and in theology.

What is scientific method? Does it guarantee a cumulative growth of knowledge? Until recently, people commonly thought that scientific knowledge increased by the smooth addition of one fact to another, the smooth refinement of an existing theory, or the smooth extension of a theory to cover new data. By analogy, ought we to expect knowledge of the Bible to progress by accumulation? Can we devise a method that will provide such progress? Or is such progress illusory even in science? Are we to expect occasional "revolutions" in biblical interpretation analogous to the revolutions in scientific theory that are investigated in some of the recent trends in the history and philosophy of science?[1] What part do underlying hermeneutical or philosophical frameworks play in influencing the results of biblical interpretation?

To answer these questions, we will have to look in some detail at theories concerned with the nature and history of scientific knowledge (chapters 2 and 3). But first, let us start with an actual example of biblical interpretation, namely, the interpretation of Romans 7. Because this passage has proved to be a difficult and controversial passage, it effectively illustrates some of the problems.

AN EXAMPLE: INTERPRETING ROMANS 7

How do we understand Romans 7, a passage that many have found some difficulty in grasping? What kind of experience is being described in verses 7–13 and above all in verses

---

[1] The key idea of revolution was introduced into the discussion by Thomas S. Kuhn, *The Structure of Scientific Revolutions,* 2d ed. (Chicago: University of Chicago Press, 1970). I comment extensively below on Kuhn's work.

14–25? And who is the "I" about whom the passage speaks? Is Paul describing his own experience or an experience typical of a whole class of people?

Through most of church history there have been disagreements over Romans 7.[2] Most interpreters have thought that Paul was describing his own experience. The use of the pronoun "I" naturally suggests this. But interpreters have also sensed that Paul's discussion here has a broader bearing. Paul would not have written at such length if he had not thought that, in some respects, his experience was typical. It was intended to illustrate something relevant for the Roman Christians' understanding of themselves, of sin, of the law, and so on.

We cannot hope to survey all the options for interpretation that have been suggested. For the purpose of illustration, it is enough for us to concentrate on the interpretations that see Romans 7:14–25 as an example of a general pattern applicable to a whole class of people. Perhaps these verses derived from Paul's personal experience, but it is not essential for us that they did. The crucial question is, What is this passage an example of? What class of people does it apply to? Does the "I" in Romans 7:14–25 stand for a believer or an unbeliever, a regenerate person or one who is unregenerate? Augustine and his followers, including Calvin, Luther, and most of the Protestant Reformation, thought that Paul was describing the conflict with sin that characterizes the life of a regenerate person, a true believer. Pelagius and some Arminians thought that this passage depicts a typical unregenerate person, or unbeliever.

A third alternative is available. Some people have seen in this passage a description of people who are regenerate but not mature, people who have not yet come into a position of

---

[2] For an introduction to the major options in the interpretation of Romans 7, see Heinrich A. W. Meyer, *Critical and Exegetical Hand-Book to the Epistle to the Romans* (New York: Funk & Wagnalls, 1884); and C. E. B. Cranfield, *A Critical and Exegetical Commentary on the Epistle to the Romans,* 2 vols. (Edinburgh: T. & T. Clark, 1975–79), 1:342–47. Note also the important contribution of Werner G. Kümmel, *Römer 7 und die Bekehrung des Paulus* (Leipzig: J. C. Heinrichs, 1929).

triumph and victory over sin. This interpretation often goes together with a "second blessing" theology, according to which sanctification, or "victory over sin," comes as a separate work of the Holy Spirit, brought about by a second step of faith. There are two kinds of Christians—those who are in the state of full sanctification and victory over sin and those who are not. Christians who do not have this victory over sin are a kind of third category intermediate between unregenerate people and ideal Christians.

How do we decide a conflict in interpretation like this one? At first glance, it might seem that we decide simply by looking at the passage and seeing which interpretation actually fits. Which interpretation is consistent with all the facts of the passage? All three interpretations above, however, *claim* to be consistent with the passage; all three claim to account for all the words and sentences in the passage.

As a next step, then, we might begin to weigh strengths and weaknesses of the three interpretations. The view that Paul is describing the experience not of an unbeliever but of a typical believer has in its favor the fact that the description of the "inner man" and the "mind" in verses 22–23, 25 appears to harmonize with Paul's statements elsewhere about Christians (e.g., Rom. 8:6; 1 Cor. 2:10), but not with his statements about non-Christians (e.g., Rom. 8:7; Eph. 4:17–18). These same facts are a problem, however, for the second interpretation.

But there are some facts on the other side. The view that the passage refers to unregenerate persons has in its favor the correspondence between Romans 7:14–15 and Paul's descriptions elsewhere of non-Christians as slaves of sin (e.g., 6:20). Romans 7:14–15 does not match Paul's descriptions of Christian freedom (e.g., 6:22; 8:4). These facts are difficult for the first interpretation to explain.

The third interpretation, that is, the "second blessing" interpretation, might therefore seem to be the best of both worlds. This interpretation creates a third category, intermediate between an unregenerate person and an ideal (sanctified) regenerate Christian, namely, an immature (unsanctified) regenerate person. By using a third category, this view avoids some of the difficulties in harmonizing the passage with statements elsewhere in Paul. But it has weaknesses of its own. Romans 7 seems to provide no clues to the reader that Paul has some third category in view. Moreover, chapter 6 seems to be talking about all Christians who have come to union with Christ, as the appeal to baptism suggests (v. 3). If so, no third category is available in the context of Romans 7. Moreover, the competing interpretations argue that no distinctive second-blessing theology is to be found in Paul or in Scripture generally. If so, the third interpretation is not viable for Romans 7 in particular.

USING CONTEXT IN INTERPRETATION

Now let us stand back for a bit and ask how we have proceeded in our analysis of Romans 7:14–25. We have looked at particular verses within the passage (vv. 22–23 and 14–15) and have seen how well the competing interpretations are able to deal with them. But in doing so, we have also had to go outside Romans 7 and look at other statements of Paul about Christians and non-Christians, slavery and freedom. These other statements need to be weighed in their own contexts to see whether they really harmonize with or contradict the chosen interpretation of Romans 7. Whether an interpretation of this chapter is viable depends on whether it is harmonizable with Paul's views as a whole.

In addition, we should not oversimplify the process of judging when an interpretation generates a contradiction or an insuperable difficulty. Each of the three interpretations has a difficulty at one point or another. If we were harsh, we would say that each generates a contradiction. But they are not necessarily all false. In fact, some people continue to advocate each of these lines of interpretation even though they are well aware of the difficulties. But they think that the difficulties are greater with competing interpretations than with their own. Hence they still endeavor to give a coherent interpretation of the difficult texts within their own viewpoint.

For example, the so-called regenerate interpretation explains that Romans 7:14–15, though similar in language to 6:20, is not saying quite the same thing. The former verses describe the real hold that the remnants of sin still have on the regenerate person until the time of glorification. In comparison with perfection, our own state might still be described as "sold under sin." This is a necessary qualification of the apparently absolute language of Romans 6. Romans 7:14–25 as a whole depicts a situation of struggle against sin, unlike the "slavery" in 6:20.

Similarly, the unregenerate interpretation endeavors to explain that the language of Romans 7:22–23, 25, though not usually applied to unbelievers by Paul, can nevertheless be used for unbelievers. Even unbelievers, it could be noted, cannot escape the knowledge of the law of God (1:32; 2:14–15).

Hence we can see that a text like Romans 7:14–15 or 7:22–23 does not just display its meaning on its sleeve, so to speak. It is not just a brute datum, about which no one can dispute. A particular verse or passage might conceivably mean something slightly different from what we think it means at first. Making sure of its meaning involves assessing context as well. What might initially appear to be a contradiction, and thus rule out one line of interpretation, might on further investigation have an explanation.

THE INFLUENCE OF OVERALL THEOLOGICAL SYSTEM AND PERSONAL EXPERIENCE

Next, we should note that people's overall theological system influences their interpretation of Romans 7. In the past, most Calvinists have advocated the regenerate interpretation; most Arminians have advocated the unregenerate interpretation. Many, if not most, adherents to second-blessing theology have advocated the second-blessing interpretation. Other combinations are possible in principle. But one can see why these influences exist.

Calvinists, for example, have a low view of the spiritual abilities of fallen, sinful, unregenerate people. Calvinists emphasize that such people are spiritually unable to turn to God and to love God unless the Holy Spirit performs a special work of regeneration to change their hearts. Calvinists are therefore reluctant to accept the positive statements of Romans 7:14–25 as descriptions of an unregenerate person.

Conversely, Arminians have a higher view of the spiritual abilities of fallen, unregenerate people. Such people have "free will." Spiritual decisions that these people make when they hear the gospel are decisive in whether they become believers. Hence Arminians are not so uneasy about attributing the positive statements in Romans 7 to unregenerate people.

Next, we should not discount the role of personal experience in influencing people's decisions about the interpretation of this passage. Some Christians are more often and more acutely aware of their failings and remaining sins. Such people can identify readily with much of the language of Romans 7:14–25 and therefore find it easy to believe that the passage describes the state of a Christian. Other Christians are more frequently aware of their joy in victory over sin. They more readily think of the contrast of their present life with their previous unbelief. They seldom dwell on the remaining areas of sin and inconsistency in their present life. Such people identify more readily with the language of Romans 6 and 8. Because 7:14–25 presents such notable contrasts with chapters 6 and 8, they are disposed to believe that it describes an unregenerate person.

Individual experience also has a role in people's attitude toward second-blessing theology. Some people have experienced a sharp transition from defeat to victory over some of their prominent sins. They may find that second-blessing theology seems to match their experience, particularly if they have undergone a radical change under the influence of hearing the teaching of second-blessing theology.

On the other hand, other people have experienced very gradual growth in their spiritual life. They have come to understand and appropriate Romans 6 and 8 gradually. But they have continued to be aware that subtle tendencies to sin still lurk in them. To them second-blessing theology seems not to match their experience. All this background of experience will influence whether a particular person finds it plausible to claim that Romans 7:14–25 describes the first-blessing stage or immature stage in a second-blessing theology.

SCIENTIFIC METHOD AND OBJECTIVITY

The interpretation of Romans 7 has been disputed for centuries. Augustine and Pelagius in the late fourth and fifth centuries were early representatives of the regenerate and unregenerate interpretations. The second-blessing interpretation arose later. But no one of the three interpretations has been able permanently to "win the day." When we look at some of the factors that go into the decision, we can begin to understand why. Differences in theological systems and in personal experience and temperament are involved.

Is there any way out of this impasse? Can the triumphs of science and the way in which science proceeds be of any value? The analogy with science might suggest to many people that the way out is through objectivity. Science, it is said, consists in a dispassionate, objective analysis of the data. The problem with the interpretation of Romans 7 is that it gets mixed up with the doctrinal commitments and personal experiences of the people doing the interpretation. The process of interpretation needs to be freed from such doctrinal commitments and personal experiences.

The historical-critical method, as developed in the eighteenth and nineteenth centuries, represented an attempt to free the study of the Bible from doctrinal commitments and to become scientific in its study. The claim to scientific objectivity was attractive, but illusory. Scholarship never takes place in a vacuum. In particular, historical research cannot be undertaken without presuppositions; the researcher must presuppose some idea of history, of what is historically probable, and of what standards to use in weighing the claims of ancient texts. Hence there is not one way of investigating history, but many, corresponding to many philosophical possibilities for one's view of history and of the possibility or actuality of God's providential control of history.

As Ernst Troeltsch incisively argued, historical research in the context of Enlightenment thought presupposed three fundamental principles.[3] According to the *principle of criticism,* no documents of the past can be accepted as authoritative; all claims about the past must be weighed by the modern critic. At most, we can arrive at a greater or lesser probability concerning the past, never a certainty. According to the *principle of analogy,* the present is the key to the past. Events of the past must all be analogous to what is possible today. According to the *principle of causality,* history is a closed continuum of events, in which every event has an antecedent immanent cause and there is no divine intervention (miracle) in history. Troeltsch saw that since the assumptions of the method already denied traditional Christianity, the results would necessarily confirm this denial.

By "historical-critical method," then, we mean historical research on the Bible, proceeding on the basis of these Enlightenment assumptions. Historical-critical method aspired to scientific objectivity, but in the nature of the case it could not succeed. In freeing biblical study from commitments to denominational doctrine, it made study subject to the philosophical commitments of rationalistic, antisupernaturalistic historiography and metaphysics and to the ethical commitments of contemporary humanism. It did not give people pristine, absolute objectivity. Furthermore, the historical-critical method did not result in any more agreement over the meaning of biblical passages. It resulted most often in more diversity and disagreement than before. It simply multiplied the number of assumptions, philosophies, and background commitments that could now exert their influence on interpretation.[4]

Is science a suitable guide, then, for biblical interpretation? Science itself, it turns out, is not purely objective and neutral. That is, science is not unaffected by commitments, assumptions, and philosophies. Until recently, most people have thought that science presented a totally objective analysis of the

---

[3] Ernst Troeltsch, "Ueber historische und dogmatische Methode in der Theologie," in *Gesammelte Schriften,* vol. 2, *Zur religiösen Lage, Religionsphilosophie, und Ethik,* 2d ed. (Aalen: Scientia, 1962), pp. 729–953.

[4] For a further discussion of historical-critical method, see the section "The Historical-Critical Method as a Revolution," in chapter 4.

facts. But recent examination of the history of science has cast doubt on this assumption. In fact, it has revealed within the realm of natural science some disputes that look curiously like the disputes over the interpretation of Romans 7. It has revealed, in a word, how people's understanding of a particular datum (e.g., Rom. 7:14–25) is influenced by a whole cluster of interpretations, assumptions, and experiences, which provide the matrix for understanding in the field as a whole. The problems with interpreting Romans 7 appear not to be such an oddity or perversity when compared with those that occur in science. Understanding this state of affairs, and learning how to deal with it, may be part of the way to a solution.

First of all, however, we must take a step backward and see what people have thought about the nature of science, scientific method, and scientific objectivity.

2

THE INFLUENCE OF NATURAL SCIENCE ON BIBLICAL INTERPRETATION

Modern science did not suddenly spring into existence, nor, once it had established itself, did it suddenly revolutionize people's thinking about the world. Yet in the long run, Western culture has been revolutionized by the impact of science. In fact, in some respects we are still embedded in a continuing process of cultural revolution. How then do we understand what science is, and how do we assess its bearing on the way that we interpret the Bible?

We should first ask whether science ought to have any influence at all on how we interpret the Bible. Biblical interpretation went on its own way, and prospered, even before modern science was in existence. Could not biblical interpretation simply continue without interaction with science?

But people cannot help making comparisons between science and biblical interpretation. The triumphs of science have proved impressive, whereas the history of biblical interpretation does not look so impressive by comparison. Physical sciences succeed in making accurate predictions. They provide integrated explanations of diverse phenomena on the basis of powerful but "simple" general principles or laws. They provide a framework for producing a continuous stream of new machines and technological innovations, increasingly useful and powerful.

The success of science and technology, even by the late eighteenth century, made intellectuals pay attention. Not only did science provide knowledge about the world; it was generating an ever-increasing amount of knowledge. By contrast, medieval and Reformational theological debates seemed to go on and on, without ever reaching a definitive conclusion. But science moved forward irreversibly. It had become not merely a body of knowledge but an engine for manufacturing more knowledge, deeper knowledge, and more solidly verified knowledge.

It is no wonder, then, that people tried to learn lessons from science. They looked especially to the physical sciences (physics, astronomy, chemistry; later, geology and biology), where the triumphs took place the earliest and have been the most thorough.[1] At least three different kinds of lessons were drawn from nineteenth-century science. The lessons differed depending on what people looked at.

USING SPECIFIC THEORIES TO TEST THE TRUTH OF THE BIBLE

First of all, some people compared specific scientific theories with views that theology had derived from the Bible, a procedure we may call evaluation using specific theories. The debates over Darwin's theory of evolution were the most notable case. Earlier, thinkers had debated whether the biblical descriptions of the sun's motion were compatible with the sun-centered astronomy of Copernicus.

Debates over specific questions of fact are certainly important in their own right. But it is not our purpose to take up such matters in this book. We should only note briefly that people responded in a variety of ways. Some (e.g., agnostics, atheists, and some deists) decided that cases of apparent conflict

---

[1] In this book, the word *science* generally refers to natural sciences, not social sciences. The natural sciences have the most widespread agreement among practitioners, and so they have naturally become the model. In fact, the desire of social sciences to attain the prestige of natural sciences influences the history of their development.

between the Bible and modern science were irresolvable. Since such people viewed science as the wave of the future, they repudiated biblical religion. Orthodox antievolutionists, however, decided that the scientific theory in question was dubious and poorly supported. Theological liberals, for their part, decided that the Bible was scientifically primitive and needed to be updated theologically. Finally, conservative theistic evolutionists thought that they could reexegete crucial biblical passages and show that the Bible did not intend to teach anything in conflict with the new theories.[2]

How do we assess this use of science? How and when do we need to use the content of a specific scientific theory as a guide for our lives? The specific theories of physical science represent impressive intellectual triumphs and provide valuable insight into the workings of the world. But they concern us more broadly only when they touch on a specific question of human values. Average people are interested in enjoying the results of technology, but few are interested in the underlying scientific theories for their own sake. They are interested in a scientific theory only if it appears to suggest answers to the meaning of their lives. Likewise, people are interested in whether the Bible is true, because such a question affects their lives vitally. Hence they ask whether science confirms or disproves the truthfulness of the Bible.

Not much within the physical sciences, however, could conceivably either contradict or confirm the Bible. Even when there is some apparent contradiction it is often easy to show that a better interpretation of the scientific theory or a better interpretation of the Bible obviates the problem. The scientific theory holds only if things continue as they ordinarily are, that is, if we exclude exceptional cases of God's dealing with the world, such as miracles. On the other side, the Bible's description of the sun's rising and of the creation of the world can be shown to be ordinary language, the language of appearances, rather than technical scientific description.

---

[2]See Bernard Ramm, *The Christian View of Science and Scripture* (Grand Rapids: Eerdmans, 1964).

Specific scientific theories do affect biblical interpretation at least to the extent that they become the occasion for reassessing the interpretation of a few passages (Gen. 1–2; 6–8). In the light of scientific claims we return to the passages to reassess whether they implied all the scientific conclusions that we have drawn from them. Likewise, biblical interpretation affects science at the very least by leading us to reassess whether all the conclusions drawn from a scientific theory are warranted, or in some cases to ask whether the theory as a whole is suspect.

Such observations do not solve all the difficulties. But they considerably narrow the scope of those that are left. The remaining difficulties must be dealt with on a technical level, by refining our scientific knowledge and refining our understanding of the Bible until we can see that they agree.[3]

BUILDING A WORLD VIEW ON THE BASIS OF SCIENTIFIC RESULTS

Besides comparing specific scientific theories with specific passages of the Bible, people drew lessons from science in a second way. They produced whole world views by extrapolating from the picture presented by physical science. Let us call this process the procedure of building a world view.

People extrapolated world views from science because physical science seemed to offer the beginnings of a whole world view, an explanation of how the whole world fit together and of the role of human beings in it. If scientific knowledge was superior to theological knowledge in its accuracy and indisputability, perhaps it was also superior in providing a platform for a total explanation. Newtonian science, in particular, offered us a world consisting of massive particles interacting with one another by means of forces calculable from physical measurements of distance, orientation, velocity, and the like.

---

[3] As I have already observed, some people may resolve the tensions by simply abandoning belief in the Bible or abandoning belief in modern science. But it is best to exercise more patience in working through the difficulties. Sometimes, as finite human beings, we may not have enough information to resolve a difficulty within our lifetime.

Some people did not hesitate to draw the conclusion: the world was a mechanistic world of particles and forces, nothing more. There was no room for God's intervention, for chance, or for human free will. Newton's theory was thereby converted into a world view, namely, the view that the world was a mechanistic, deterministic collection of particles in motion.[4]

Though Darwin's theory of evolution has already been considered as a case of using a specific scientific theory, it was also used as the platform for a world view. "Social Darwinism" extrapolated Darwin's claims about survival, fitness, and evolution into the area of human social interaction.[5] Even those who did not go all the way into social Darwinism often saw Darwin's theory as a complete explanation of life—an explanation that eliminated God. Of course, Darwin's theory could be narrowly construed as a technical scientific hypothesis for explaining the fossil record and the existing distribution of species. But the cultural atmosphere made it convenient to invoke the theory in support of much broader conclusions. Many people, for religious, philosophical, and ethical reasons, wanted to legitimize a naturalistic view of the world. Darwin, by eliminating the need for miracles in the origin of life, gave crucial support to these philosophical longings.[6]

How do we evaluate these efforts? Do physical sciences provide us with a world view? Does this world view agree with the world view offered in the Bible? To a certain extent, one might say that science and the Bible both provide us with only pieces of a world view. The Bible here and there provides

---

[4]It should be noted that early scientists like Newton and Boyle operated within a Christian world view and did not think that their theories undermined the reality of God's rule over the world. See John Dillenberger, *Protestant Thought and Natural Science: A Historical Interpretation* (Westport, Conn.: Greenwood, 1977); and Francis Oakley, *Omnipotence, Covenant, and Order: An Excursion in the History of Ideas from Abelard to Leibniz* (Ithaca: Cornell University Press, 1984).

[5]Richard Hofstadter, *Social Darwinism in American Thought, 1860–1915* (Philadelphia: University of Pennsylvania Press, 1945); Thomas H. Huxley, *Evolution and Ethics, and Other Essays* (New York: Appleton, 1898).

[6]Loren Eiseley, *Darwin's Century: Evolution and the Men Who Discovered It* (Garden City, N.Y.: Doubleday, 1961).

information touching on scientific questions, but it does not answer all our questions about the way in which the physical world functions. Conversely, physical science, understood soberly and modestly, does not answer questions about human values and destiny, nor does it give information on supernatural acts that may be an exception to God's normal government of the world.[7]

But many people did not remain content with these limitations. They boldly extrapolated from physical science to comprehensive world views, deriving mechanistic determinism from Newton and the naturalistic world of evolutionism from Darwin. Such world views, because they pretended to offer a total explanation, competed with the Bible's claims. They did not simply contradict a single passage of the Bible, as a specific scientific theory might. Rather, they contradicted the Bible globally, by offering an alternative world view, an alternative set of values, and an alternative explanation of origins and destiny.[8]

This second use of science (as a platform for a world view) is thus even more significant theologically than the first. It offers deeper challenges and potentially more destructive conclusions because it can threaten biblical religion as a whole. Nevertheless, it is not our purpose to pursue this difficulty. The most adequate answers are to be found in writings on Christian approaches to science. A number of Evangelicals have put forward ways of integrating the scientific task as a whole into a biblical world view.[9]

---

[7] See Charles Hummel, *The Galileo Connection: Resolving Conflicts Between Science and the Bible* (Downers Grove, Ill.: InterVarsity, 1986); Del Ratzsch, *Philosophy of Science* (Downers Grove, Ill.: InterVarsity, 1986).

[8] The feeling that modern science contradicts the biblical view of the world is far from dead. Rudolf Bultmann claims, "It is impossible to use electric light and the wireless and to avail ourselves of modern medical and surgical discoveries, and at the same time to believe in the New Testament world of spirits and miracles" ("New Testament and Mythology," in *Kerygma and Myth*, ed. Hans Werner Bartsch [New York: Harper & Row, 1961], p. 5).

[9] See Hummel, *Galileo Connection;* Robert Ream, *Science Teaching: A Christian Approach* (Philadelphia: Presbyterian & Reformed, 1972); Russell Maatman, *The Bible, Natural Science, and Evolution* (Grand Rapids: Baker, 1970); Ratzsch,

BUILDING AN EPISTEMOLOGY ON THE BASIS
OF SCIENTIFIC METHOD:
THE EXAMPLE OF KANT

Finally, science was used in a third way, namely, as a source of insight about the nature of knowledge itself. Let us call this the procedure of building an epistemology, or a philosophical theory of knowledge.

This third way is in many respects the most promising. As we observed, the procedure of using specific scientific theories is useful only when a specific theory happens to touch on issues of human concern. Most of the time it does not. The procedure of building a world view is questionable, since one must extrapolate science beyond what has been verified. On the other hand, the procedure of building an epistemology relies on the undoubted success of science as a means for producing knowledge. Even if science does not include all knowledge, its success surely contains lessons that apply to all knowledge.

The classic example of using science as a platform for epistemology is to be found in Immanuel Kant.[10] Kant at an early point in his life followed the rationalistic, deductive approach of Leibniz. In opposition to this rationalism, Hume defended an empiricism that started with pure events and did not assume that they were connected, merely that they sometimes occurred together. As Kant testified, Hume "awakened him from his dogmatic slumber." Kant then rejected rationalism. He was convinced that there was no guarantee that phenomena would turn out to be connected in the way that a

---

Philosophy of Science; Vern S. Poythress, *Philosophy, Science and the Sovereignty of God* (Nutley, N.J.: Presbyterian & Reformed, 1976); idem, "Science as Allegory," *Journal of the American Scientific Affiliation* 35 (1983):65–71; Herman Dooyeweerd, *A New Critique of Theoretical Thought,* 2 vols. (Philadelphia: Presbyterian & Reformed, 1969); idem, *The Secularization of Science* (Memphis: Christian Studies Center, 1979); Hendrik van Riessen, *Wijsbegeerte* (Kampen: Kok, 1970); Stanley Jaki, *The Road of Science and the Ways of God* (Chicago: University of Chicago Press, 1980).

[10]For further discussion of Kant, see Royce G. Gruenler, *Meaning and Understanding: The Philosophical Framework for Biblical Interpretation* (Grand Rapids: Zondervan, forthcoming).

rationalist supposed. And yet, Hume's own empiricist solution was also inadequate. Hume's world contained no intrinsic connection between individual events. Hence Hume could not account for the reliability of scientific knowledge. The rationalistic approach of Leibniz did not lead to fruitful science either.

Kant therefore endeavored to provide an epistemology that was adequate to science and that also preserved room for religion. Kant accepted the obvious fact that science did provide knowledge. Kant's task was then to provide an epistemology that accounted for the success of science. Science arose from a combination of empirical data (Hume's concern) and rational inference (Leibniz's concern). An adequate epistemology would do justice to both these elements.

Kant's solution was to say that, whatever we observed empirically, we observed necessarily in terms of categories presupposed by the human mind. Inner experience (experience even within one's mind, without looking at the world) was necessarily experience against the background of time. Outer experience was necessarily experience in a framework of both time and space. To these categories of time and space one could also add the categories of quantity and causality, which are basic to physics. The empirical element in science was accounted for, since human experience was experience of a world outside that was not always predictable. On the other hand, the rational element in science was accounted for, since human experience necessarily conformed to the preestablished categories of the mind. The world of phenomena was not pure confusion, as Hume had it. Rather, it was necessarily a world of time, space, and causality, and this was the foundation for sure knowledge.

On the surface, Kant's solution seems attractive. In fact, however, a closer examination shows that it provides both too little and too much for the needs of physical science.[11] On the one hand, it provides too little. Suppose we agree that it shows the necessity of conceiving the world in terms of the categories of time, space, causality, and quantity. This result still does not

---

[11] See especially Jaki, *Road of Science*, pp. 112–27.

constitute scientific knowledge, nor is it an adequate basis for guaranteeing that we can obtain scientific knowledge.

After all, any particular physical theory, such as Newton's laws, Boyle's law, and Dalton's law, furnishes predictions to the effect that the world will behave in one way, not another, within the general framework of time, space, and causality. To say that there are causal connections (Kant) is not yet to say what kind of causal connections there are (Newton). To say that everything has a cause (Kant) is a long way from saying that all bodies attract one another with a force given by the formula $F = GmM/r^2$ (Newton). Kant's epistemology guarantees only that there is necessarily a cause for any event. It does not allow anyone to say that the cause must necessarily be what Newton says it is. In fact, in Kant's scheme the particular way that the world is, within the conceptual framework of causality, is ultimately not predictable. It is contingent. The phenomena presuppose things in themselves that cannot be predicted beforehand. A tightly formulated general law, like Newton's, predicts something that Kant says cannot be predicted. Hence Kant still is unable to explain why a simple formula like $F = GmM/r^2$ should hold true all the time, while other formulas do not.

Second, Kant's epistemology provides too much for the needs of science. Namely, it dictates to science assumptions that may not turn out to be factually correct. Kant's categories of time, space, and causality are most naturally understood as actually implying a particular theory of physical time, space, and causality. In Kant's environment, these categories seemed to imply a linear absolute time scale, Euclidean space, and determinism in the realm of physical causes. These things were virtually part of people's intuitions about space, time, and causality. In turn, these intuitions or views were compatible with Newton's theory of gravitation, so people were content with them at the time.

In the light of better scientific knowledge, however, physicists today are not willing to agree with Kant. Physicists now realize that the ideas of absolute time, Euclidean space, and determinism were all assumptions about the world that might be either true or false, not presuppositions that were necessarily true. Kant did not take into account two facts. First, the psychic experience of time, space, and causality by the ordinary person is not the same as the time, space, and causality that may be most suitable to physical theory. Intuitions derived from psychic experiences may or may not be immediately useful in physical theory. Second, intuitions themselves can be reformed. In Kant's time, "space" meant Euclidean space. Given a line and a point not on the line, one and only one line could be drawn through the point, parallel to the first line. But modern physicists, confronted with coherent alternatives to this scheme, have had their intuitions changed. For them it is not obvious (in fact, it is false) that physical space is Euclidean.

Kant's solution, then, did not really correspond well with the nature of science. It did not even fit the specifics of Newtonian science. And it fit even less well the developments of the twentieth century that were destined to supersede Newton. But Kant's philosophy had enormous impact nonetheless. It was accepted because of its promise in the field of philosophy rather than because of its accuracy in the realm of science.

For Kant, in fact, epistemology became the basis for philosophy as a whole. By means of his reflection on the categories of the human mind, Kant specified what could and could not be the object of knowledge. And this pronouncement virtually determined what could and could not be part of the world. From Kant until the twentieth century, epistemology has been the key to philosophy as a whole. Hence Kant's work was not just an epistemology. It was a full-blown philosophy. It provided its own world view.

In Kant, then, epistemology leads to a world view. Hence we cannot rigidly separate the third use of science (building an epistemology) from the second use (building a world view). Epistemology is a part of a world view, and in post-Kantian philosophy often it is the principal part. Nevertheless, a rough-and-ready distinction between these two ways of using science is useful. The second use wants to read off a world view directly from the picture of the physical world presented in current

Figure 1. Deriving Broader Conclusions from Science

1. Evaluation using specific theories

Scientific theory   Biblical texts

    ↓ Deduction   ↓ Interpretation

Specific prediction   Factual claim

                comparison

2. Building a world view

Cluster of scientific theories

    ↓ Extrapolation

World View

3. Building an epistemology (theory of knowledge)

Scientific method

    ↓ Epistemological analysis and generalization

Epistemology

    ↓ Inferences concerning objects of knowledge

World View

scientific theory. The third use, the more philosophical use followed by Kant, wishes to reflect primarily on *how* scientists know what they know, rather than on *what* they know. From this reflection it derives general conclusions about the nature of human knowledge, and from there it derives further conclusions about what there is to know. (See figure 1.)

Kant provides us with a cautionary lesson here. When we seek to derive from science an epistemology or a world view, we may produce a world view that in fact does not really match science but that may be heavily motivated by philosophical and religious needs.

BACONIAN AND POSITIVISTIC UNDERSTANDING OF SCIENCE

Not everyone followed Kant, however. The scientists, perhaps, followed him least of all. Alongside Kant and his followers there continued a longstanding empirical tradition going back to Sir Francis Bacon (1561–1626). Bacon and scientists after him assumed that science studied the real world. Science did not just study "phenomena" in a Kantian sense; it did not just observe a world whose order derived from the categories of the human mind already read into it in the act of perception. The world was "out there," and scientists had the task of discovering its laws.

Scientists also assumed that the world was regular and had its laws. Hume's philosophical skepticism made him doubt whether there were real laws. But practicing scientists ignored Hume's theoretical problem. The laws were there. People could discover them by a series of steps laid out by Bacon. The steps came to be known as the scientific method.

1. Gather data.
2. Formulate a general rule (hypothesis) accounting for the data.
3. Derive predictions from the hypothesis.
4. Check the predictions by making experiments.
5. If the predictions prove true, give the hypothesis the

status of a (tentative) law. Laws are always subject to further testing.

6. If a prediction proves false, return to step 1 and attempt to derive another hypothesis.[12]

As we shall see in the next chapter, these steps are not an adequate representation of how scientists actually proceed. The six steps are only an idealization. They leave out some crucial aspects of scientific research. But until about 1962, most scientists and philosophers of science thought that scientific progress occurred in this manner. And in reality, the above six steps are close enough to the truth to enable people to ignore the discrepancies for a long time. For the sake of clarity, we will call the six steps the Baconian scientific method.

Baconian scientific method, then, does not match what scientists actually do. But until recently it did match what nearly everyone, scientists and nonscientists, *thought* that the scientists were doing (or ought to be doing). Moreover, there was no doubt that science produced impressive results. Hence the conclusion was not far behind: Baconian scientific method was the preferred instrument for producing impressive results.

It was attractive to try to assimilate the practice of biblical interpretation to the practice (or supposed practice) of science. One important area of this assimilation was historical reconstruction.[13] Biblical interpretation involves a lot of historical work. Accurate grammatical-historical interpretation involves assessing the historical environment in which biblical books were written, determining the human authors and original readers of each book, understanding relevant cultural and geographical information, and so on. Historical reconstruction cannot be an exact science, but it can benefit from some of the

---

[12] This conception of scientific method was further formulated, refined, and set in the context of a comprehensive philosophical viewpoint by the school of logical positivism, beginning in the early twentieth century. See Ratzsch, *Philosophy of Science,* pp. 21–39. For our purposes, we may ignore the variations in conception and concentrate on the common features.

[13] For a more thorough discussion of the role of historical investigation in biblical interpretation, see volume 5 in the Foundations of Contemporary Interpretation series (Grand Rapids: Zondervan, forthcoming).

methodological care exercised in the natural sciences. Hence Baconian scientific method was applied.

Some adjustments were clearly necessary. Historical reconstruction is concerned with single events in the past rather than a general law (see step 2). But one can still formulate hypotheses about a past event. One cannot perform experiments on history in the same way that one can perform experiments on frogs. But checking one's hypothesis for consistency with data not originally included could serve as a substitute for experimental confirmation in step 4.

The application of Baconian method to historical investigation seemed reasonable. But the development of the historical-critical method showed that it was not always innocent. The historical-critical method assumed, just as scientists supposedly assumed, that the same laws governed the past, present, and future and that tight causal laws governed the sequence of events.[14] Historical research conducted on this basis already assumed that the miraculous was impossible. At this point, something out of the mechanism of post-Newtonian science, or out of the rationalistic world view of the Enlightenment, slipped into the very methods of research in biblical study. And having slipped into the methods, it naturally dictated the conclusions.

One qualification to this picture is necessary. The historical-critical method took its clue not so much directly from natural science as from the general intellectual developments of the Enlightenment and the refinement of standards for intellectual research of all kinds. But these general intellectual developments were in turn influenced by the example of science. In one way or another the natural sciences influenced biblical studies.

Of course, the historical-critical method, with its naturalistic assumptions, was not the only way to do historical research. Orthodox theologians and biblical scholars continued to believe in the supernatural. They believed that the world was governed by God for rational purposes. This belief provided a

---

[14]Troeltsch, "Ueber historische und dogmatische Methode."

basis for historical research just as much as did belief that the world was governed by rational laws untouched by God.

In addition to the controversy over the canons of historical research, the Baconian ideal had an influence on biblical interpretation and on theology. Biblical scholars were interested in making their own work more rigorous. It was easy to say that theology had to become scientific, and it did so by following the Baconian scientific method. Charles Hodge, for example, lays out what he considers to be proper method in theology by explicitly invoking the analogy of scientific method.[15] The individual texts of the Bible are the data, which the theologian/"scientist" uses inductively to formulate principles in the form of general doctrinal truths. The principles are to be checked for their consistency with the whole Bible.

Baconian scientific method had its effect even on people who did not consciously endeavor to assimilate their work to the methods and standards of science. The method presupposed a certain relation between data, hypotheses, scientific laws, and the sciences that codified the laws into coherent wholes. Underlying the Baconian method were the following assumptions:

1. Data are hard facts, about which there is and can be no dispute.
2. Hypotheses arise from seeing a pattern in the data and making an inductive generalization. The generalization says simply that all cases fit the observed pattern. Seeing a pattern is an act of insight that cannot be perfectly controlled, but once a pattern is seen, the generalization follows.
3. Predictions from a hypothesis are derived by simple deduction from the hypothesis itself.
4. Discarding or retaining a hypothesis is a relatively simple matter, depending merely on whether the additional experimental data support it.
5. Confirmed hypotheses are added to the existing list of

---

[15] Charles Hodge, *Systematic Theology*, 3 vols. (Grand Rapids: Eerdmans, 1970), 1:9–17.

general laws. Progress in science consists in piecemeal additions to the list of known laws.

These assumptions summarize the heart of an inductive, positivist view of scientific knowledge. According to this view, knowledge has two parts—individual *bits of hard data,* which are the indisputable basis for knowledge, and *general laws,* which are its superstructure. Each law summarizes a pattern found inductively in the data. The laws group together the data that they generalize. But except for the grouping of data under laws, all of knowledge is fundamentally atomistic. Each bit of data stands on its own feet, and each law in the existing list of laws stands on its own feet over against other laws.

Moreover, it could also be said that scientific method has two parts. In the inductive part, one gathers data and generalizes to hypotheses. In the deductive part, one derives predictions and discards disconfirmed hypotheses. The production of hypotheses cannot be completely mechanized, but all the other steps are in principle purely objective.

The above assumptions represent only a simplified summary, but do express an important tendency in thinking about science. And this tendency has also infected exegesis and theology. In exegesis, this view of knowledge says that the individual words and morphemes are the hard data. The statements about the meaning of paragraphs and discourses are the laws. Hypotheses about meaning are discarded when they do not agree with some of the data (i.e., when they do not account for some word, phrase, or sentence). Progress in exegesis means adding to the store of correct interpretations of individual passages.

In systematic theology, individual passages of the Bible are the data, and the laws are general theological truths. Theological hypotheses are discarded when some passage contradicts them. Progress in theology means adding to the store of general truths derived from the Bible.

Both in natural science and in biblical interpretation, this inductive view of knowledge is inadequate. Worse, it leads to distortions and hindrances in the progress of knowledge. To see why, we will first look at the revisions that have taken place in the understanding of scientific method (chap. 3). We will then ask what implications we can draw for biblical interpretation (chaps. 4–11).

3

THOMAS KUHN AND CONTEMPORARY DISCUSSIONS OF SCIENTIFIC DISCOVERY

At the end of the nineteenth century, scientists had reason to be confident about their achievements. Newton's theory of gravitation had proved successful. It not only gave accurate predictions of the movements of planets but did so with an aesthetically pleasing, mathematically elegant set of equations. More important, it furnished a fundamental framework in which all further scientific investigation could be integrated. To be sure, scientists had still not thoroughly explored and mastered every potential area of investigation in physics, let alone every area of biology. But they could confidently expect that those yet-to-be-explored areas would harmonize with Newton's framework.

THE SCIENTIFIC REVOLUTIONS OF THE TWENTIETH CENTURY

The twentieth century rudely shattered this complacency. Within a period of thirty years, two revolutions in physics overturned Newton's universe in a way that a nineteenth-century physicist would have said was impossible. In 1905, Albert Einstein published his first paper on the special theory of relativity. This theory contradicted the fundamental assumption of Newton that measurements of length in space, length in time, and mass of particles are independent of the person's situation who does the measuring. Since space, time, and mass were fundamental to Newton's entire theory, the whole view of the physical universe had to be rethought.

The second revolution, the quantum revolution, began with Max Planck's papers on radiation in 1900.[1] Planck postulated that light was emitted in fixed quantities of energy, rather than being emitted in a simple continuous stream. Planck's idea remained an oddity in physics for more than twenty years. The corpuscular character of light that Planck's theory implied could not be fully reconciled with many other phenomena showing the interference patterns of waves. But to this oddity were gradually added other oddities showing a similar pattern. Neils Bohr in 1913 succeeded in explaining atomic spectra on the basis of quantum ideas, but this account was in one respect still odd: there was no framework capable of thoroughly reconciling particle and wave aspects of the behavior. Finally, in 1925 and 1926, Werner Heisenberg and Erwin Schrödinger produced formulations accurately predicting atomic-energy levels. Schrödinger's formulation ("wave mechanics") depended on representing atomic electrons by waves corresponding to fixed quantities of energy, that is, quantized levels of energy. The universe that Newton had assumed to have continuous levels of energy was found to be discrete. Worse, this universe, at an atomic level, behaved not like a particle, not like a wave, but in a way showing features of both. Causality itself seemed to function oddly at an atomic level. In order for the equations of quantum mechanics to hold, it was argued, some events must be innately unpredictable or indeterminate.

Both special relativity and quantum theory invalidated Newton's equations. Furthermore, they showed that the basic intuitions behind Newton's universe were invalid. They produced a picture of the universe that went contrary to intuition.

---

[1] See Sir Edmund Whittaker, *A History of the Theories of Aether and Electricity,* rev. ed. (New York: Harper, 1960), 2:81; George Gamow, *Thirty Years That Shook Physics: The Story of Quantum Theory* (New York: Dover, 1966).

According to special relativity, events at high speed deviate in strange ways from what we are accustomed to in our everyday world. According to quantum theory, events on a very small scale deviate in strange ways. The quantum revolution proved, if possible, even more unsettling because it was impossible to picture the underlying realities. They could be accurately described only in terms of equations that provided no good intuitive picture of the world. Relativity and quantum theory both spawned further developments that were nearly revolutions in their own right and moved the world of physical theory even further away from the old world of Newton.

First, as a development of relativity, Einstein published in 1915 his "General Theory of Relativity." In this theory he expanded the theory of special relativity to include an account of gravitation. In the new theory mass and energy corresponded to curvature in the very structure of space and time. Newton's view of the universe, by contrast, had assumed that space and time were flat. And it had assumed that gravitation was a "real" force, not something that could be equated with the structure of space and time itself.

Second, in the area of quantum theory, Max Born and Werner Heisenberg introduced an alternative to Schrödinger's formulation, called matrix mechanics. The details of this proposal are not important for our purposes. At a deep level it was, in fact, mathematically equivalent to Schrödinger's formulation. But Heisenberg for the first time explicitly formulated the uncertainty relations of quantum mechanics, namely, mathematical statements implying that one cannot measure a particle's position and momentum simultaneously.

Reflection on the uncertainty relations and on the phenomena of wave/particle duality spawned a philosophical interpretation of quantum theory, namely, the "Copenhagen interpretation." This school said that, in many atomic situations, key quantities like position and velocity were not fully defined in a classical sense until an experiment was performed measuring them. The measurements in the experiment in effect "forced" a particle to take a determinate position or velocity. This view was more radical than several alternatives. For instance, one could have said merely that we as observers did not know what the actual value was (as a Newtonian might have said). Or one could say that we could never in principle know the actual values of all the variables, because measurement of one value inevitably disturbed the others (this conclusion was a result of quantum theory, not of Newton, but it was still fairly safe). But the Copenhagen interpretation said that talk about definite actual values, independent of measuring them, was virtually meaningless.[2]

After Heisenberg and Schrödinger, refinements in quantum theory have continued to appear. These refinements have made the nature of quantum description ever more esoteric. Heisenberg's and Schrödinger's work has now been surpassed in turn by Dirac's relativistic quantum mechanics, quantized field theory, quantum electrodynamics, and quantum chromodynamics. One does not know what theories will appear in the future on the border of knowledge.

After these two revolutions, one could still claim in retrospect that Newton's theory worked as a first approximation. Relativity was a refinement of Newton in the domain of high velocities. Quantum theory was a refinement in the domain of very small physical systems. This qualification helped people to preserve the idea that scientific advance consists simply in adding to the body of known truths.[3]

But it was difficult to deny that some other things were going on as well. Both relativity and quantum theory challenged not primarily some poorly established hypothesis or some theory just beginning to be established, but the very best

---

[2]See, for example, Norwood Russell Hanson, "Quantum Mechanics, Philosophical Implications of," in *The Encyclopedia of Philosophy,* ed. Paul Edwards (New York: Macmillan, 1967), 7:41–49. For a nonmathematical explanation of quantum theory, see John Gribbin, *In Search of Schrödinger's Cat: Quantum Physics and Reality* (New York: Bantam, 1984). Slightly more advanced is J. C. Polkinghorne, *The Quantum World* (Princeton: Princeton University Press, 1984). A thorough exploration of the issues is to be found in the more technical book by Max Jammer, *The Philosophy of Quantum Mechanics: The Interpretation of Quantum Mechanics in Historical Perspective* (New York: Wiley, 1974).

[3]See Kuhn, *Structure of Scientific Revolutions,* pp. 98–102.

and most firmly established physical theory (Newton's). And they offered the challenge at the very basis of the theory, by disputing the very ideas of measurement and reality interwoven with every single experiment.

Hence the existence of these revolutions raises questions about the naïve inductive view of scientific research discussed in the previous chapter. Are scientific data and scientific laws atomistic? Does scientific progress consist simply in adding more data and adding more laws to the list of approved laws? Or if such a picture is not quite right, is it enough to add a footnote to the effect that occasional pruning of old laws may replace them with more accurate versions of the same? The revolutions produced by the theory of relativity and quantum theory, however, included changes in the shape of physical theory of a most radical nature.

THOMAS KUHN AND THE REVOLUTION IN HISTORY AND PHILOSOPHY OF SCIENCE

The watershed in thinking about scientific progress occurred in 1962. In that year Thomas S. Kuhn published *The Structure of Scientific Revolutions,* in which he rejected the classic view of science, the view associated with Baconian scientific method. Kuhn argued that science did *not* advance merely by a step-by-step inductive method.[4] Research on specific problems always took place against the background of assumptions and convictions produced by previously existing science. In mature science, this background took the form of "paradigms," a cluster of beliefs, theories, values, standards for research, and exemplary research results that provided a framework for scientific advance within a whole field. Since the word *paradigm* has come to be used in several different senses, we will instead use the phrase *disciplinary matrix.*[5] Newton's fundamental work,

---

[4]Ibid., pp. 1–4.

[5]In the first edition of Kuhn's work, he failed to distinguish two main senses of his use of the word *paradigm.* In the first sense, it designates "the entire constellation of beliefs, values, techniques, and so on shared by the members of a given community" (p. 175). In the second sense it designates "concrete

Philosophiae Naturalis Principia Mathematica, generated just such a disciplinary matrix within the field of natural science in general and physics in particular. Newton's work was an exemplar, a concrete research result that suggested a way of problem-solving for a large number of unsolved problems. At the same time, as people reflected on the implications of Newton's work, they obtained from it not only a prime example of a successful theory but a framework that suggested further questions, experiments, and generalizations building on and within the overall theory. Newton's theory evolved, then, into a disciplinary matrix for subsequent research.

In chapter 2, we analyzed Baconian scientific method as involving six fundamental assumptions. Over against these assumptions, we may summarize Kuhn's view in a series of counterassumptions:

1. Data are never "hard facts," completely independent of any theory. What counts as data depends on the disciplinary matrix, or framework of assumptions, that scientists use. All data is "theory-laden." It already presupposes, in its very status as data for a given experiment or a given theory, that the universe is organized in a way compatible with the assumptions of the science as a whole. The current disciplinary matrix affects how scientists make observations, what they think the observations actually measure, and what kinds of data or experiments are relevant to the outstanding open questions in their field.

2. Hypotheses do not arise from making a generalization in a vacuum. Rather, they arise from the combined influence of the overall disciplinary matrix in the field, detailed experimental results, the structure of theories in related areas that may suggest analogous solutions in

---

puzzle-solutions" that provide models for further research (ibid.). It is usually not too hard to disentangle these two senses within Kuhn's book. In the discussion below I use *disciplinary matrix* for the first sense, *exemplar* for the second sense. Kuhn himself has now recommended this terminology (pp. 182, 187).

the area currently under scrutiny, and expectations generated by the ruling disciplinary matrix as to what types of theory are most likely to be successful.

3. One cannot simply deduce a prediction from an isolated hypothesis. Predictions from a hypothesis depend not only on the hypothesis itself but on a surrounding body of theory specifying how the hypothesis is related to any particular experimental setup. One must also include here "observation theories," theories about any specialized apparatus used in measurements and the meaning of those measurements.

4. Discarding or retaining a hypothesis is almost never easy. Experiments can go wrong for a large number of reasons. Some unforeseen interference may not have been excluded from the experiment. Any one of a group of hypotheses or laws helping to relate the given hypothesis to the experiment may be invalid. One of these may have to be discarded, but a single experiment, or frequently even a whole series of experiments, does not indicate which of a series of connected, mutually dependent hypotheses is incorrect.

5. Most important, science does not advance merely by adding confirmed hypotheses to an existing atomistic list of laws. The laws of a given field of science are related to one another in a coherent way. Additions and subtractions affect the whole. Moreover, there can be times of "revolution" when the whole body of knowledge is recast.

Kuhn is particularly stimulating on the subject of this fifth point, the question of scientific progress. In this area, Kuhn distinguishes between at least three kinds of situations in the development of a particular scientific field. The first is "immature" science. In this situation, the field of investigation for the science is poorly defined. Different workers in the field dispute the kinds of data that are relevant to their field, the purpose of the investigation, the shape a finished theory will have, and the kind of tests that confirm or disconfirm the theory. Investigators are casting about for a fundamental insight that will bring order into a disparate field. In immature sciences, it is not clear how one measures progress. People do experiments and gather data, but because of the unsettled character of the field, it is seldom clear whether their work will make a lasting contribution. Kuhn thinks that the social sciences, for the most part, may still be in this state.

The second kind of situation is that of normal "mature" science. A particular science becomes mature when some investigator or group of investigators advances a fundamental theory, including supporting data, that proves clearly superior. This theory becomes an exemplar, a key research result that largely determines the whole disciplinary matrix for subsequent research. It suggests a whole line of experiments, a "research program."[6] The theory explains and organizes a significant body of data. In addition, it confirms its promise by engendering a whole line of experiments that refine, extend, and confirm the theory and that link it with other existing theories. The success of the new disciplinary matrix inaugurates a period of "normal science," devoted to "puzzle-solving."[7] Most of the scientists working in the field devote themselves to small puzzles, the remaining areas of investigation where the overall disciplinary matrix already suggests lines of questioning and the forms of hypotheses that might solve the puzzle.[8]

As long as the scientists in a field continue to solve the

---

[6] Imre Lakatos, not Thomas Kuhn, introduced the phrase *research program* (see Lakatos, *The Methodology of Scientific Research Programmes*, ed. John Worrall and Gregory Currie [Cambridge: Cambridge University Press, 1978]). This phrase expresses insights similar to Kuhn's.

[7] See Kuhn, *Structure of Scientific Revolutions*, pp. 35–42. Kuhn also calls this activity "mop up work" (p. 24).

[8] Kuhn subclassifies the puzzle-solving into three types (pp. 25–30). The first type works at a more accurate and more comprehensive determination of quantities that "the paradigm [disciplinary matrix and exemplar together] has shown to be particularly revealing of the nature of things" (p. 25). A second type works on those areas where the most direct, definitive experimental checks on the theory can be performed. A third type consists in work attempting to extend or articulate further the disciplinary matrix. All of these types of investigation are closely regulated by the disciplinary matrix.

puzzles that they find for themselves, they go forward in a way that superficially resembles the Baconian inductive ideal. They add small bits of generalization to the existing body of generalizations. There are always some remaining anomalies, or areas where explanations have not been produced. Here and there are some potentially embarrassing data that do not seem to be compatible with the existing disciplinary matrix. Nevertheless, as long as people are making progress in the puzzle-solving, they assume that incremental advances in the field (or in some neighboring field) will eventually enable them to see the compatibility of the anomalies with the disciplinary matrix.

The third situation is that of "extraordinary" science, leading to scientific revolution. Revolution occurs when an existing disciplinary matrix is replaced by a new one incompatible with the original. A revolutionary situation first arises when anomalies in a particular field cannot easily be ignored. The anomalies begin to fall into patterns that show an order of their own. More and more tinkering with the disciplinary matrix is necessary in order to produce any kind of rational summary of the anomalies. Inelegant, complex, unmotivated hypotheses arise to account for the anomalies. As more and more energy is devoted to working on the anomalies, tinkering with the reigning disciplinary matrix leads people to produce different versions of the disciplinary matrix. The disciplinary matrix itself no longer looks so unified as it once did.[9]

In this situation people are willing to search about more broadly, looking for better solutions. In the process they are willing even to challenge ideas traditionally associated with the existing disciplinary matrix. Eventually they stumble upon an alternative approach, inexact at first, but appearing to offer some possibility of dealing with the anomalies. This approach is refined, enhanced, and reformed in order to increase its accuracy and the scope of data accounted for. If the process continues, this new approach generates a disciplinary matrix of its own. A fight then ensues between adherents to the old disciplinary matrix and those holding the new as to which

[9] See, for example, ibid., p. 83.

matrix is to be used in the future development of science. In this period, it is difficult for adherents of the two disciplinary matrices even to communicate well with one another, because they may have different standards for what counts as data and different standards as to what sorts of explanation have the most promise.[10]

Kuhn also notes that, if no satisfactory solution arises, even after prolonged effort and radical attempts to generate alternative explanations, people may fall back on the existing disciplinary matrix and treat the anomalies as an intractable area reserved for future generations. In this case, the period of extraordinary science has not generated a revolution but has collapsed back into normal science, working with essentially the same disciplinary matrix as before.

A SPECIFIC ILLUSTRATION
OF KUHN'S THEORY

The study of electricity provides an example of the process of change in science. According to Kuhn, in the first half of the eighteenth century there was no standard theory of electricity. There was no clear exemplar to bring coherence to the progress of research. Instead, "there were almost as many views about the nature of electricity as there were important electrical experimenters, men like Hauksbee, Gray, Desaguliers, Du Fay, Nollett, Watson, Franklin, and others."[11] In such a stage of immature science, there is as yet no standard disciplinary matrix in the field. Some of the theories of electricity of the time regarded "attraction and frictional generation as the fundamental electrical phenomena." Others regarded attraction and repulsion as equally fundamental. A third group regarded electricity as a fluid that ran through conductors. In each case the idea of which phenomena were fundamental directed the concentration and goal of the research.

The preparadigm stage came to an end with Franklin's

---

[10] See, for example, ibid., pp. 109–110, 198–204.
[11] Ibid., pp. 13–14.

work *Electricity,* which became the exemplar for future research. It proved its superior promise by encompassing all the phenomena within its scope.[12]

Subsequent to Franklin's time, the field of electrical research represented a field of normal science. Franklin's theory was elaborated, refined, enhanced, and extended. Scientists no longer debated about the fundamental nature of electricity or the fundamental directions that research should take. They could therefore concentrate more on esoteric phenomena; they could study in great detail the phenomena that the theory indicated were of greatest significance. No individual scientist needed to return and reconstruct the whole field from its foundations up. The resulting specialization made the literature on electricity less accessible to the general public but meant efficiency in making progress within the specialization.

The theory of electricity has since been normal science. However, according to Kuhn, normal science may at times be interrupted by revolutions in theory. These revolutions may take place within a small specialty (such as studies of diamagnetism) or within a broader field. Kuhn is not explicit, but inspection of the history of electricity subsequent to Franklin suggests a series of mini revolutions in small areas. Kuhn does mention explicitly a revolution introduced by James Clerk Maxwell in the second half of the nineteenth century.[13] Maxwell's electromagnetic theory introduced "displacement current" and other ideas difficult for his contemporaries to digest. The triumph of his theory therefore took time, during which some adherents to older views were converted and some were displaced by a younger generation.[14]

---

[12] Franklin provided a theory that "could account with something like equal facility for very nearly all these effects and that therefore could and did provide . . . a common paradigm [exemplar]" (ibid., p. 15).

[13] Ibid., pp. 107–8.

[14] See Whittaker, *History of the Theories,* 1:254: "It was inevitable that a theory so novel and so capricious as that of Maxwell should involve conceptions which his contemporaries understood with difficulty and accepted with reluctance."

4

IMPLICATIONS OF KUHN'S THEORY FOR BIBLICAL INTERPRETATION

What do we make of Kuhn's theory of scientific revolutions? Kuhn's book has had mixed reception by philosophers and historians of science.[1] Such a reception is just what we might expect. Kuhn claims that his book is part of a revolutionary change in the historiography of science.[2] A revolutionary change will meet resistance at the beginning.

PRELIMINARY EVALUATION OF KUHN

My own opinion is that Kuhn is on the right track, that he does bring to light many aspects in the development of science concealed by the reigning philosophy of science and by textbook remarks about the history of science.[3] Moreover, there are reasons for thinking that much of what Kuhn says is applicable to scholarly communities of any kind, not just to science. Hence his ideas should be applicable to biblical

---

[1] See Gary Gutting, ed., *Paradigms and Revolutions: Appraisals and Applications of Thomas Kuhn's Philosophy of Science* (Notre Dame: University of Notre Dame Press, 1980); Imre Lakatos and Alan Musgrave, eds., *Criticism and the Growth of Knowledge* (Cambridge: Cambridge University Press, 1970); Ian Hacking, ed., *Scientific Revolutions* (Oxford: Oxford University Press, 1981).

[2] Kuhn, *Structure of Scientific Revolutions,* pp. 1–3.

[3] On the role of textbooks in concealing revolutions, see ibid., pp. 136–43.

interpretation. But not everything that is true of science is true of biblical interpretation. Kuhn himself is just as concerned with the uniqueness of science as he is with its similarities to scholarly research of other kinds.[4]

What relevance, then, does the activity of science have for biblical interpretation? More particularly, what relevance might Kuhn's ideas have? To answer this question, we must determine to what extent biblical interpretation does or does not have analogues to the processes that Kuhn describes in science. Whether or not Kuhn is right about science is somewhat secondary. Even if he is right, the same patterns and principles might not hold in biblical interpretation. Even if he is wrong about science, he may be right when we apply his claims to biblical interpretation.

ROMANS 7 COMPARED WITH IMMATURE SCIENCE

Let us, then, look at a particular example: the interpretation of Romans 7. Recall from chapter 1 the conflict between three different interpretations of this passage. This conflict looks vaguely like the situation that Kuhn describes in immature science, when a scientific field has not produced a single unified paradigm or disciplinary matrix based on a successful exemplar.

The most striking similarity between the two cases lies in the unresolved disputes between schools. In immature science the investigators may be grouped into a number of competing schools. Each school has a different idea about the fundamental nature of the field and about the lines of explanation along which understanding will come. Similarly, in the interpretation of Romans 7 there are two schools, what I have called the regenerate school of interpretation and the unregenerate school. Later in history, these two were eventually joined by the second-blessing school. Just as in immature science, progress is possible in a sense within a school.[5] Members of the regenerate

---

[4] Ibid., pp. 208–9.
[5] See ibid., pp. 160–63.

school can refine the understanding of individual verses, draw out the implications of these verses, expand on the connections that the verses have with other parts of the Bible, and so on. But there are two hindrances to progress, just as there are in immature science. First, if the existing school turns out to be wrong, all its work will later be judged as just a false trail, and not progress at all. Second, the existence of competing schools means that a good deal of the energy of any one school is spent in reexamining its own foundations and trying to show that its foundations are superior to those of competing schools. Only when everyone in the field agrees on the foundations can there be concentration on the details and progress on those details.

We should not be surprised at these similarities between immature science and the situation in interpreting Romans 7. The similarities arise largely because schools are composed of human beings aiming to understand some subject. In this situation people inevitably behave in ways that they think will most enhance understanding. Enhancing understanding involves interacting with their peers and with competing schools along the lines that we have just laid out—the same lines that scientific schools follow, according to Kuhn.

But there are also certain important differences between the schools of thought concerning Romans 7 and the schools in immature sciences. The former do not really have social cohesiveness, for we have simply classified people into schools for convenience in classifying the different interpretations. By contrast, the schools in immature science, the schools that Kuhn has in mind, have inner social cohesiveness. They form natural subgroups within a community of investigators. The community is bound together, first of all, by common interests in the subject matter. Because of the common interests, letters and articles will be sent back and forth, and there may be some degree of personal acquaintance. Each subgroup will, of course, be more intensely united because of the similarity of their views of the subject they are investigating.

The analogue of scientific schools within biblical interpretation would seem to be not the different schools of thought on Romans 7 but the schools of theology, such as Calvinists,

Arminians, and advocates of second-blessing theology. These schools are schools within a larger community, consisting of all biblical scholars and theologians. These schools and the broader community in which they exist both have demonstrable social cohesiveness. The schools are social groups with communication back and forth; they have common goals and some common standards of evaluation.

The problem of interpreting Romans 7 is one research problem on which the community works. The preferred approach to dealing with the problem varies from school to school, just as it might in an immature science.

There is one more difference between interpretation of Romans 7 and immature science. Typically, in immature science, there may not even be agreement as to which phenomena are part of the field of investigation or which phenomena are most revealing of the nature of things. Different investigators concentrate their research on different areas. The effect may be reminiscent of the story of blind men investigating an elephant; one described the trunk, one the side, one a leg, one the tail, and one an ear. As long as no one has a clue to the true extent of the phenomena that may be amenable to explanation by a unified theory, and as long as no theory has succeeded in dominating the field, the boundaries of the field itself are understandably uncertain.

In biblical interpretation and theology, however, the field of investigation is fixed. The schools in theology—Calvinists, Arminians, and second-blessing theologians—can pretty much agree on their subject matter. All study Romans 7, all take into account the same lexical and grammatical information, and all use the same standard lexicons and grammars. All agree on the relevance not only of Romans 7 but of other passages of Romans, the rest of Paul's epistles, and ultimately the rest of biblical teaching as a whole.

But here we can begin to see that this measure of agreement is not always achievable. Roman Catholics include in their list of canonical books some books and additions not included in the Protestant list. Traditional Roman Catholics also allow a role for church tradition and for papal teaching such as

Protestants would not allow. Some critical scholars want to have a canon within the canon, perhaps Paul's epistles or Paul's teaching on justification, in terms of which they think it possible to judge other teachings of other parts of the Bible as substandard. Cultic groups like the Mormons and Christian Scientists have their own holy books supplementing the Bible. Clearly these different groups do not have the same standards or the same field of investigation.

Even if we concentrate on Evangelical Protestantism, which accepts the Bible as its standard, there are some differences. Confessional churches also give a role to their confessions. The confessions are "secondary standards," while the Bible is the primary standard. The confessions are in theory fallible and correctable, whereas the Bible is not. But confessional theologians are committed to paying attention to their confession. They respect it because it embodies the collective wisdom of their denomination and of past generations, as these generations have been illumined by the Holy Spirit. Confessional theologians will not lightly conclude that the Bible contradicts their particular confession.

The advantage of this stance is that it restrains arbitrary and facile innovation. It protects biblical interpreters from reinventing old heresies—that is, old schools of investigation that have been found to be dead ends. Its disadvantage is that it may keep investigators from acknowledging new truth that they find in the Bible. Moreover, to the degree that a confession actively functions as a standard for judging an interpretation of the Bible, it produces a difference of atmosphere in interpretation for the school that holds it. Thus there may be an attenuated sense in which the Calvinists, the Arminians, and the second-blessing theologians, or at least those who are bound to a doctrinal statement, do not completely agree on the very field of investigation or the methods by which to do the investigation.

THE POSSIBILITY OF REVOLUTION IN
BIBLICAL INTERPRETATION

According to Kuhn's scheme immature sciences become normal, mature sciences when they develop a single, stable disciplinary matrix. The unified disciplinary matrix includes a key exemplar, a research result in the form of a theory with supporting experimental evidences. By its aesthetic appeal, its superiority in explanatory power, and its fruitfulness as a basis for further research, this exemplar wins more and more adherents. Eventually it dominates the field. Some older scholars in the field never accept the new theory. They have too much confidence and too much investment in the old. But eventually they die or are effectively excluded from the research community. If they do research, they do it using other ground rules, and the main portion of the community simply pays no attention to their results.

It is natural to ask whether we might find something similar in biblical interpretation. As long as theology is divided into schools of Calvinists, Arminians, Roman Catholics, and so on, it is like immature science. Can a revolution bring unity into this field, similar to the unity in a mature science? If so, how do we set such a revolution in motion?

Some people have already tried to apply Kuhn in a similar way to social sciences. For instance, the science of psychology presently includes a number of competing schools that maintain different principles and fundamental frameworks for research. Behaviorism, Freudianism, Marxism, and humanism each offers itself as a base for psychological research. This situation is immature science. Hence people point to Kuhn and argue that psychology must become mature. To do so, psychology must first decide on a unified approach. And then people offer their own approach as the basis.

But this response is a misunderstanding of Kuhn. Kuhn does not think that one can have a revolution any time one wants. Immaturity is precisely the state in which no one disciplinary matrix, no one theory, is able to win everyone's allegiance. One cannot simply impose allegiance but must wait for the arrival of a theory with clear superiority or at least a promise of superiority. The progress of time, and the refinement of the theory, then makes its superiority more and more evident and irresistible. Or perhaps the progress of time makes things no better: attempts at refining the theory succeed well in some cases but not so well in other cases, and the new theory may not uncover order in new sets of phenomena in any more promising ways than the old ones did. A revolution that one hopes will take place on the basis of a new theory may not take place.

When we look more closely at the history of biblical interpretation, we can see some patterns of revolutionary breaks, followed by periods of stability and consolidation. Western theology after Augustine largely built on Augustine and the ancient creeds. These sources, in a sense, formed the exemplars for biblical and theological scholarship through most of the medieval period. Something of a crisis was provoked by the absorption of Aristotelian philosophy in the late medieval period. More and more anomalies were found through the efforts to assimilate and harmonize the new philosophical influences with the Augustinian framework. The work of Thomas Aquinas was an answer to this problem. Thomas's continuities with Augustine make it unclear whether he essentially refined Augustine or whether he produced a revolutionary triumph. (And one must not forget that Thomas never won over the allegiance of the whole Western theological community to the extent that Augustine did.)

The Reformation period confronts us with a theological revolution in a sense. Humanistic interpretation introduced a new disciplinary matrix for the study of the Greek classics and the Bible. This framework produced more and more anomalies in the relation between the meaning of the Bible and the teaching and practice of the church. In addition, the late medieval synthesis in theology broke down as philosophical reflection found more and more anomalies in theological reasoning itself. The increasing number of anomalies, the finding of anomalies in areas of importance, and the finding of patterns in the anomalies all showed more and more the unsatisfactory character of piecemeal tinkering within the framework of dominant late-medieval synthesis. The time was ripe for theological revolution, which, in the broad sense, did come. People abandoned the old disciplinary matrix for theology. But no one new disciplinary matrix won everyone's allegiance, and so theology divided into multiple schools.

To describe the medieval and Reformation periods in this way is undoubtedly a vast oversimplification. And yet there seems to be an insight here. As we already observed, it appears that human beings in communities, interested in understanding a subject and solving its problems, are bound to proceed in similar ways in both science and theology.

THE HISTORICAL-CRITICAL METHOD AS A REVOLUTION

A second revolution in biblical interpretation took place with the growth of the historical-critical method. This revolution was again provoked by the increasing prominence of anomalies in theology of two main kinds. First, the doctrinal differences within the Reformation and the theological schools associated with them did not disappear. Each school refined its arguments. Each position maintained that it was right, that its arguments were fully persuasive, and that it had adequately refuted the competing positions. Over time, people could not help wondering whether each position was maintained partly by prejudice. The anomaly here was the inability of the schools to deal with prejudice. Moreover, the differences between theologies were all the more painful because they were one factor in wars. Overcoming the differences seemed to be critically important. At the same time, it was impossible to solve the differences using existing modes of argumentation.

Second, developing interest in study of human nature and culture gave people awareness of religious differences between cultures. It was easy to ask whether human reason could be used to sort through religious differences and perhaps to adjudicate between theological schools. Philosophical reason, used by sinful people, wished to dictate what God was like and what divine revelation was like. Deism arose and was at odds with what the Bible claimed. For those attracted to deism, the conflict represented an anomaly.

The historical-critical method arose within this framework as an attempt to produce a scientific exegesis and an objective historical study of the biblical documents. The same standards were to apply to the Bible as applied to any secular historical document. The theological commitment of the practitioner was not to intervene. By this means one eliminated the "prejudice" contained in the interpreter's background within one of the theological schools or a church associated with a fixed theological school.

The historical-critical method did represent a revolutionary challenge in the Kuhnian sense. It altered, sometimes subtly, sometimes radically, the entire framework in which exegesis had been carried on. Under the old framework, or disciplinary matrix, exegesis took place by comparing a passage with other passages and trying to arrive at an interpretation that harmonized them all. Now, exegesis found tensions and contradictions wherever it could, seeing these as clues to the different sources behind the final text.

The old framework required that the exegete inquire concerning the meaning of the text in its final context within the canon. Now, the exegete inquired into the history behind the text, the history of story telling, composition, combination, deletion, and editing that led to the final text. In the old framework, the exegete found guidance from the church's confession and doctrinal commitments. Now, the exegete was systematically to ignore such guidance. In the old framework, the exegete accepted the supernatural claims of the Bible at face value. Now, the exegete sifted such claims in the same way as the claims of any other historical document were evaluated. This position typically meant that the exegete rejected supernatural claims out of hand, because a scientific historian assumed that the history was composed of natural causes.

The contrast between old and new frameworks shows the potentially revolutionary character of the historical-critical method. It was a method capable of altering a person's perspective and method of attack on *all* of the subject. To a certain degree, one might even say that it changed the boundaries of the subject. The canon was no longer separated from other religious writings. Christianity in the first century rather than the New Testament might be the primary focus of research.

The contrast also shows that, even though the post-Reformation theologies were divided, they shared to some degree a common hermeneutical framework. That unified framework, the old framework, still provided something of a disciplinary matrix for coherent research communities. The historical–critical method introduced an alternative disciplinary matrix.

The historical–critical method triumphed within academic circles. It won over enough adherents to make possible a new unified basis for proceeding with future research. As in the case of scientific revolutions, the people who were not willing to conform to the new standards of research were gradually excluded from participation in the scholarly community.

Of course, the historical–critical method never triumphed so completely as did the Newtonian revolution or the Einsteinian revolution in physics. Some orthodox, supernaturalistic theologians and biblical scholars remained, and some held academic positions in major universities. The results differed from country to country. Roman Catholic countries were for a long time little affected by historical–critical innovations. Germany was more thoroughly antisupernatural than England, England more than the United States.

Kuhn's comments about the later stages of a scientific revolution to some extent also characterize the historical–critical revolution. A revolution creates a divide between people who accept it and those who do not. The two groups have different conceptions of the important problems, standards, and goals of research; they make different assumptions about the truths that are "assured results" and the kinds of evidence that are relevant. Once some people are sure that the revolution has triumphed, they waste little time debating with other people who are still not convinced. Those who are convinced find that it is a waste of time to continue debating the foundations of the field. It is time to go on with research on detailed problems, because the disciplinary matrix provides agreed-upon foundations for the field.

After the historical-critical method had gained sufficient adherents, new faculty hired in university departments of theology were therefore bound to be those who showed their promise partly by adherence to the method. Hence after a time, people not adhering to critical method would effectively disappear from academic positions. To some extent, students had to conform to the method to pass courses and receive degrees. The same is still true today in some cases. Evangelical students have sometimes been told frankly by a scholar in the historical-critical tradition, "You don't belong in the doctoral program here. You can't be a scholar unless you are willing to study the Bible critically." Such a comment sounds harsh. But it is no more harsh than a physicist's telling students that they do not belong in a doctoral program as long as they do not accept the special theory of relativity.[6]

The practice of exclusion also takes place in scholarly publication. Articles are accepted in scholarly journals of biblical interpretation only if they conform to the standard of the method. Today Evangelical scholars often write articles for publication in academic journals that move within the historical-critical tradition. For the article to be accepted, however, they must write about a subject in which sufficient methodological agreement is possible. Some of the topics most important to Evangelicals, such as the authority of Scripture, the resurrection of Christ, and the deity of Christ, are difficult to write about because in most cases the Evangelical finds it important to appeal to a high view of biblical authority, which is just what

---

[6]Although I think that special relativity is basically right and the historical-critical method is basically wrong, the issue here is not whether some disciplinary matrix is right or wrong in an absolute sense. The issue is whether the existing community of scholars has, for one reason or another, valid or invalid, come to be assured that its position is so clearly right as to need no further discussion. Such people characteristically think that only obtuseness or intellectual failure could prevent someone from working in their framework.

the historical-critical method denies in principle, at its very foundation.

Finally, the practice of exclusion takes place in the publication and reading of scholarly books. Individual adherents to the historical-critical method often think that reading Evangelical books would be a waste of time. Often it *is* a waste of time, at least under the assumption that the historical-critical method is right. Some books by Evangelicals on some topics use methods sufficiently close to historical-critical standards to be of interest. But a good many do not. When a book uses different standards, its results will be less interesting. The situation seems parallel to the situation in science. Scientists will never see the point of reading works of a previous (uninformed) generation or contemporary works of what they consider pseudoscience.

The effect holds also for whole seminaries and university departments of theology. If a seminary or department is committed to the historical-critical tradition, it will in all probability have few, if any, books by Evangelicals on its reading lists. For this tradition, those books are a waste of time for the students as well as the professors. Evangelical works, it is said, are less "scholarly." But of course most such books are bound to be less scholarly because they are judged by the historical-critical standard. The result is that the next generation of students is mostly unaware that there is a reasoned alternative to the historical-critical tradition. Even those who for personal religious reasons would like to be Evangelicals think that this position is intellectually untenable.

To some extent, however, Evangelicals have been less scholarly by any standard. Evangelicals, because of their views on the spiritual and eternal importance of biblical knowledge, have a natural concern to produce suitable popular and semipopular literature. In addition, the triumph of the histori-cal-critical revolution has meant that few Evangelicals were *allowed* to be scholars in the first place. Churches who still wished to hold to orthodox doctrine could and did react to this situation with anger and withdrawal, which often produced anti-intellectualism. Such an attitude in the church discourages the next generation from doing scholarship. And so the unhappy situation continues. Today, fortunately, we see a resurgence of Evangelical scholarship of high caliber in the United States, Britain, and South Africa.[7]

In summary, the history of the historical-critical method shows that there are many striking similarities between the social structure of knowledge in biblical interpretation and in science. Comparable elements include the structure of an immense discipline with many schools, the problems of debating the foundations and boundaries of a field, the transition to a single dominant disciplinary matrix in a mature discipline, the effects of social exclusion on people who do not share this matrix, and the ability of the dominant framework to enable research to progress to details.

Evangelicals have repeatedly refused to accept some of the crucial assumptions of the historical-critical method. They have done so even though this method has become the dominant disciplinary matrix in biblical interpretation. Is this refusal really as obtuse as a refusal to accept special relativity?

---

[7] See Mark A. Noll, *Between Faith and Criticism: Evangelicals, Scholarship, and the Bible in America* (San Francisco: Harper & Row, 1986).

5

DIFFERENCES BETWEEN BIBLICAL INTERPRETATION AND SCIENCE

The similarities between the historical-critical revolution and revolutions in natural science might make us wonder whether sheer obtuseness has prevented Evangelicals from accepting the whole historical-critical package. It is important, however, that a significant number of people reject the historical-critical method. There is a reason for this rejection, however illogical and irrational it may appear to people who adhere to the reigning method.

WHAT COUNTS AS SUPERIOR BIBLICAL INTERPRETATION?

We may assess what makes a particular disciplinary matrix superior by following the logic of Kuhn's analysis of scientific revolutions. Kuhn does not merely assert that a revolution happens when a new disciplinary matrix displaces an old one. He shows why and how this revolution takes place in a community of scientists. First, a growing number of anomalies arise that are seen as important, and a growing number of researchers devote their energies to solving the anomalies within the existing disciplinary matrix. As attention is concentrated on anomalies, more and more are discovered. If repeated attempts to deal with the anomalies produce solutions that are less than satisfactory, some researchers begin to explore more radical alternatives. Variants of the disciplinary matrix arise. Then some researcher, typically one new to the field, finds a fundamentally new way of looking at some of the anomalies. Even though this new way is incompatible with parts of the reigning disciplinary matrix, it seems to have some promise. As it is developed into a full-blown theory, it eventually proves superior in explaining the anomalies, is able to explain most of the phenomena explained by the old theory, and above all suggests a whole pattern of research that shows promise of uncovering and explaining large bodies of additional phenomena that the old theory could not handle. When the new theory begins to show itself superior in this way, more and more scientists in the field get on the bandwagon.

However, Kuhn notes that, in the earlier stages of the revolution, the new theory may not allow quantitative explanation any better than the old one did. Copernicus's sun-centered astronomy did not at first provide quantitative predictions any more accurate than Ptolemy's. At the beginning it is not easy to decide which approach is superior, because people are trying to guess how well the alternative approaches will solve problems in the future. Typically there is no one point in time when one can say that now, and not before, the new theory is decisively proved and the old one refuted.[1]

Now let us take this approach to the revolution introduced by the historical-critical method. Was this method, as a disciplinary matrix, superior to the older approach of reading the Bible as a harmonious source of doctrine? In what way is it superior? What problems did it promise to solve better?

The proponents of the historical-critical method might have listed the following benefits:

1. It offered the promise of superseding the old doctrinal disputes by providing an objective standard for interpretation.

---

[1] See the similar observations in Lakatos, *Methodology of Scientific Research Programmes.*

2. It abandoned belief in the supernatural, which was an embarrassment in the age of reason.
3. It promised to explain, rather than gloss over, differences, tensions, and "contradictions" between parallel passages.
4. It promised to give insight into the history of each text's origin.

The last point is particularly important, because the cultural atmosphere was moving toward the view that, in human affairs, historical explanation was the correct, satisfying type of explanation to seek.[2]

Point (2) and, in part, point (4) touch on philosophical and cultural influences that did not affect all biblical interpreters equally. Similar philosophical influences can be found during scientific revolutions. In times of extraordinary science, people's evaluations of anomalies and alternative theories are often influenced by philosophy and other cultural forces.

From the standpoint of theologians who were firmly committed to the supernatural, point (2) made the historical-critical method inferior, not superior. But why were some people firmly committed to the supernatural, and why should this commitment be any different than firm commitments that some scientists have to elements within the old, prerevolutionary disciplinary matrix?

Here we touch on at least one important difference between natural science and biblical interpretation. Biblical interpretation has things to say more directly about human life and about the life of the individual practicing interpreter as a whole person. Religious commitments are some of the deepest commitments that people have. People have emotional investments in their religion that often exceed the investments they have in a vocational interest such as doing research or doing science. Hence they more vigorously resist giving up these commitments.

[2] See James Barr, "The Interpretation of Scripture, II. Revelation Through History in the Old Testament and in Modern Theology," *Interpretation* 17 (1963): 193–205.

How, then, do we rate the relative potentials of various approaches to studying the Bible? Evidently one factor in our evaluation should be a requirement that biblical interpretation say something about what we should believe and not merely do research on the Bible and on ancient religion. The historical-critical method, within the twentieth century, has now come under criticism from within for its failure to produce from its researches anything preachable. Many opponents as well as a few proponents of the historical-critical revolution saw this problem from the beginning.[3]

The requirement, then, that research on the Bible eventually relate to the needs of the church was unlike the requirements within a discipline of natural science. Not surprisingly, more radical representatives of the historical-critical method called for a complete separation from the church in order to achieve scientific status. But too many biblical scholars were interested in the Bible partly because of its personal, existential value. The pure separation may have been an ideal for the historical-critical method, but it was never achieved.

THE EXPERIENCE OF GOD: A FUNDAMENTAL DIFFERENCE BETWEEN BIBLICAL INTERPRETATION AND SCIENCE

But we have still not penetrated quite to the heart of the matter. The Bible claims to be what God says.[4] Within the

---

[3]Opponents of the historical-critical method were, of course, well aware of the antisupernatural bias of the method and saw that it would leave us without a supernatural gospel. But even some proponents like Troeltsch saw the implications: the method guaranteed the dissolution of orthodox doctrinal Christianity as it had existed up to that time (see Troeltsch, "Ueber historische und dogmatische Methode").

[4]This claim is, of course, disputed by many adherents to the historical-critical method. Occasionally, however, one can find critics admitting that some parts of the Bible do have similar claims. The critics, on their part, simply disagree with the claims. See F. C. Grant, *Introduction to New Testament Thought* (Nashville: Abingdon, 1950), p. 75; Benjamin B. Warfield, *The Inspiration and Authority of the Bible* (Philadelphia: Presbyterian & Reformed, 1948), pp. 115, 175–77, 423–24.

precritical disciplinary matrix, people heard God speaking to them as they read the Bible. All of the Bible testified that what God said could be trusted and that it ought to be trusted, even in situations that seemed to throw doubts on it. God was the Lord. Obedience to Him, including trusting what He said, was a supreme religious duty. Whenever conflicts arose, the apostles' priority was clear: "We must obey God rather than men" (Acts 5:29). This commitment ruled out sifting, criticizing, doubting, or contradicting any part of what the Bible said. Moreover, it ruled out rejecting miracles or the supernatural aspects of the world, to which the Bible clearly testified. In a word, it ruled out the historical-critical method from the beginning. Conversely, the historical-critical method ruled out true biblical religion from its beginning.

Two things must be noticed about this process. First, the Bible made supreme claims about its own authority. People adhering to biblical religion had religious and emotional investments in it in ways formally similar to the emotional investments of non-Christians in non-Christian religions or the investments of Enlightenment secularists in humanism or rationalism. But biblical religion (and ultimately non-Christian religions and secularist idolatries as well) requires supreme loyalty and supreme emotional commitment. Hence the refusal to give up one's religion, seen from the outside as stubbornness in the face of facts, is, from the inside, loyalty in the face of temptation to treason. By their very nature, supreme loyalties or basic commitments are supreme. They do not tolerate rivals.[5] The Bible requires adherents to biblical religion, if necessary, not merely to suffer intellectual puzzlement and dissatisfaction at not having key answers, scorn for being unscholarly, or loss of vocation by being ostracized, but to submit even to torture and death for the sake of being loyal to God. In short, the commitments to biblical religion are more serious than any scientific commitment could be.

---

[5] For elaboration, see John M. Frame, "God and Biblical Language: Transcendence and Immanence," in God's Inerrant Word, ed. John W. Montgomery (Minneapolis: Bethany Fellowship, 1974), pp. 159–77.

Second, people really did hear God speaking in the Bible. Or (as a skeptic would say) they thought that they did. The historical-critical method ignored from the outset the heart of the Bible, because it ignored, and in effect denied, this experience. But not everyone who read the Bible had this same experience. Different people, looking at the same Bible, heard different things. Naturally this discrepancy produced a division within scholarship. Scholars who heard God refused to follow the historical-critical method. Whatever its other advantages, the historical-critical method had a crucial disadvantage: it falsified the whole nature of the field to be investigated. Scholars who did not hear God embraced the historical-critical method because, whatever its current unsolved problems, it approached the Bible at last without the old dogmatic commitments.

Of course, things were a bit more complex. Some people who once thought that the Bible was God's Word and that they heard God speaking to them in its words later came, under the influence of the debate, to reinterpret their experience. Some people who once did not hear God in the Bible, under the same influences, later came to realize that He was speaking those words.

What do we make of this situation? I agree with the explanation found in the Bible itself. Two forces, two persuasive powers, are at war with one another in human hearts.[6] Sometimes the forces exert themselves in the clamor of popular debate, sometimes in the cultural atmosphere and world view of a society, sometimes in the careful arguments of scholars, sometimes in the appeals of orators, and sometimes in the quietness of individuals alone, weighing their own desires and hunches. God the Holy Spirit is one force, testifying to the truth. The sinful human heart is the other force, desiring to be like God, to reach its conclusions independent of all other

---

[6] Christians and non-Christians participate in spiritual war in fundamentally different ways, since they belong to opposite kingdoms (1 John 5:19). But neither Christians nor non-Christians are consistently loyal to their own side. Christians give in to sin and Satanic temptation, while non-Christians do not escape the knowledge of God and of good (Rom. 1:20, 32).

authority. And this sinfulness is the platform for the seductions of Satan and his preternatural assistant demons.

Some people, but not all, come to new birth by the Holy Spirit. When their hearts are enlightened, they see and hear in a way that other people, bound in sin, do not see and hear. In principle, this change may affect all of life, because all of life belongs to God. But obviously some areas and aspects of life touch more closely on people's obedience to God or to Satan. Studies of humanity are, on the average, closer to the issues of the heart than are studies of subhuman nature. Studies of the Bible, the Word of God, are typically closer to the heart of the matter than studies of economics or sociology.

KUHN'S RELEVANCE IN THE MIDST OF THE DIFFERENCES

It would seem, then, that biblical interpretation is different from natural sciences. Some of its differences it shares with social sciences, or with any kind of research that studies some aspect of human experience. Other differences arise because it touches on basic commitments and on the heart of the spiritual conflict in this world.

In spite of such differences, Kuhn uncannily describes the situation in a scientific revolution in a way reminiscent of religious conversion. Revolutions are "changes of world view," which "cause scientists to see the world of their research-engagement differently."[7] To demonstrate this claim, Kuhn finds it useful to distinguish between "stimuli," the physical forces impinging on the human body, and "sensations," the items we are actually aware of. The stimuli are the same, but the sensations are the same only for people who have had the same upbringing and education. Changes in world view affect the manner in which we interpret the stimuli. To this observation I might add that most people, myself included, do not experience sensations either, if this word connotes in a

---

[7] Kuhn, *Structure of Scientific Revolutions,* p. 111. See further pp. 111–35, 191–207.

narrow way bits of experience associated each with a single sensory apparatus, cleanly isolated from everything else. Only people influenced by an empiricist world view learn to isolate sense bits from a holistic human experience of wholes. Others with a different world view know that we experience a unified world. We experience God as well, since created things testify to Him (Rom. 1:21; Ps. 19:1–6).

Whatever one might say about world views in general (and it is worth reflecting on Kuhn's views on this subject), Kuhn's observations fit the situation introduced with the rise of the historical-critical method. Practitioners of the method and opponents of the method did not see the same thing when they examined the Bible. One saw a human product of the social evolution of religious ideas. The other saw God speaking. Their methods of investigation were correspondingly different.

Actually, in the history of interpretation there are not merely two interpretive positions, one a thoroughgoing historical-critical method and the other a thoroughgoing belief in all the Bible's claims because of its divine authority. Many people struggled to find intermediate positions that accepted the historical-critical method as one means of attaining a more accurate knowledge of a uniquely "inspired" but fallible biblical message. Others claimed to follow the historical-critical method wholeheartedly but introduced extra religious or philosophical assumptions of their own. Others in the Fundamentalist camp maintained the full authority of the Bible but denied the profitability of scholarly reflection. In a sense the anomalies generated by the Enlightenment crisis of Christian faith and autonomous reason generated not two disciplinary matrices but a whole spectrum.

6

DISCIPLINARY MATRICES IN BIBLICAL INTERPRETATION

It is time now to take stock of what we have observed about biblical interpretation as an academic discipline.

THE DYNAMICS OF INTELLECTUAL DEVELOPMENT IN BIBLICAL INTERPRETATION

I note first that there are communities and subcommunities of people engaged in intensive intellectual reflection concerning biblical interpretation. I am not thinking here of the community of all members of a church or a denomination, whose concerns and interests are usually different from those interested in solving intellectual problems in biblical interpretation. I focus on communities consisting of scholars working on some common concerns and communicating with one another. A disciplinary matrix in biblical interpretation consists of the "constellation of group commitments" of such a community.[1] Unity within interpretive communities depends on just such a disciplinary matrix, a network of shared assumptions, methods, standards, and sources. Sometimes a particularly outstanding work in theology may set the pace for the future of theological reflection. Augustine's theology became the exemplar for the

---

[1] Kuhn, *Structure of Scientific Revolutions*, p. 181.

medieval period, and Calvin's theology became the exemplar for one post-Reformation school (Calvinism). At some times and places in the history of the church, a great deal of unity has existed; at other times, a number of competing schools have vied for dominance, each offering a somewhat different version of a preferred disciplinary matrix.

Over time, it is possible for one disciplinary matrix to be replaced by another. Such an event might be labeled an interpretive revolution or a theological revolution. The Reformation and the rise of the historical-critical method are examples of revolutions. The description of such revolutions can to a great extent follow the lines of Kuhn's description of scientific revolutions. In fact, Kuhn indicates that his own idea of revolution is originally borrowed from the history of other fields:

> Historians of literature, of music, of the arts, of political development, and of many other human activities have long described their subjects in the same way. Periodization in terms of revolutionary breaks in style, taste, and institutional structure have been among their standard tools. If I have been original with respect to concepts like these, it has mainly been by applying them to the sciences, fields which had been widely thought to develop in a different way.[2]

We might expect this commonality simply because human communities interested in giving explanations in a field and solving the problems of the field are bound to behave in similar ways, whatever the field. If one line of explanation (one exemplar) seems promising, they stick with this line of explanation until they start having problems with it. Anomalies multiply. Then some more adventuresome souls tinker with the existing disciplinary matrix. If a resolution is not found, more radical alternatives are tried. If one of these seems to promise success, more and more people convert to the new alternative. A revolution thus begins. We have applied this analysis to both science and biblical interpretation.

I note, however, that revolutions in biblical interpretation

---

[2]Ibid., p. 208.

never seem to be as successful as those in science. A generation after Einstein's work, it is impossible to find a pure Newtonian. But it is still possible to find Augustinians, Thomists, and people who reject the historical-critical method.

TYPES OF DISCIPLINARY MATRICES IN BIBLICAL INTERPRETATION

Revolutions in biblical interpretation, or changes in disciplinary matrix, can be more or less major, or radical, in character. Changing from medieval theology to Calvinism, or from Calvinism to Arminianism, represents a major change. But through the change some things remain similar. All three theologies agree that the Bible is God's Word. What the Bible says, God says. The historical-critical revolution, in challenging the common assumption of all three of these theologies, represented a more radical revolution than a change from one to another of the three. Since the Bible was the primary source for theology, changing the status of the Bible and the way that it was investigated would radically change theology as a whole.

Moreover, the disciplinary matrix of a theological community includes a network of many different kinds of assumptions and values. We have summaries of theological truths in confessions and doctrinal statements. We have assumptions about the source of theological authority, whether authority is ascribed to the Bible, to experience, to doctrinal standards, to church tradition, or to some combination of these. We have assumptions about the methods to be used in interpreting the Bible, the relation of human authors to God, the relation of the Old and New Testaments, and so on. We have standards for the kinds of argumentative procedures to be used, such as the *Sic et Non* of Abelard, the syllogisms of Aristotle, or the logic of Petrus Ramus. We have assumptions about the responsibility of biblical interpreters to the church. We have assumptions about human nature and its ability to penetrate theological truth.

Conceivably, a minirevolution in biblical interpretation might touch one of these areas more than the others. Thus we might distinguish between hermeneutical revolutions, doctrinal revolutions, and revolutions in authority. But since many revolutions in practice have touched to some degree on several of these areas at once, any classification is likely to be artificial.

It might be more fruitful to think of the size of the community that is revolutionized by a particular change. Today we can distinguish, at least in a rough and ready way, the subcommunities of Old Testament scholars, New Testament scholars, systematic theologians, church historians, homileticians, specialists in Christian education, specialists in counseling, missiologists, and the church at large. A change that was revolutionary within a given field might cause minor changes, but not revolution, in sister fields. Kuhn notes that the same is true in natural science.[3] Finally, we must remember that the change of a single individual from one disciplinary matrix to another is a kind of revolution for that person. For example, a Calvinist might become an Arminian, or an adherent of orthodox theology might turn to the historical–critical method. Kuhn calls this kind of personal revolution a conversion.[4] Obviously this type of conversion does have some epistemological similarity to religious conversion in the ordinary sense. But for the sake of clarity I will call this type of personal revolution an alternation.[5]

A religious conversion to Christianity is the most radical possible change. Such conversion affects one's whole world view. Even from a sociological or anthropological point of view, the change is more radical than changes of theology within the Christian faith. Moreover, we must say that the change is not merely intellectual, or even primarily intellectual. It involves a new set of beliefs, but it also involves a new life. Theologically speaking, we are dealing here with the religious root of human existence. Is a person for God or against Him? Is a person reconciled to God or still alienated? This question points to roots deeper even than a change of world view, since

---

[3] Ibid., p. 181.

[4] Ibid., p. 204.

[5] The term is from Peter L. Berger and Thomas Luckmann, *The Social Construction of Reality: A Treatise in the Society of Knowledge* (New York: Doubleday, 1967), pp. 157–61.

changes of world view can take place in a conversion from one non-Christian religion to another, or a transition (by either a non-Christian or a Christian) from tribal to modern Western culture.

The next most radical change is a change in world view. By *world view* I mean the network of assumptions, values, customs, and ways of coping with the world that are common to one's culture or subculture, held largely unconsciously. The final qualification here is important, for a world view is not simply a self-consciously adopted philosophy or theory of the world. It is what one assumes without realizing that one is even assuming it. A change from the supernatural world view of medieval society or the world view of a tribal society to the naturalistic, mechanistic world view of the modern West is such a change. It involves changes in self-consciously held beliefs, to be sure. But it involves changes also in things that one thought were impossible to change.

Less radical than changes in world view are changes of theological systems. Changes in theology from Roman Catholic to Protestant or from Arminian to Calvinist are examples. Such changes represent revolutions for a systematic theologian. For specialists in exegesis, changes in one's view of the historical setting or one's view of the author's genre and purpose would often have a sweeping effect analogous to a systematic theologian's change of dogmatic system. Changes in hermeneutical method might result in revolutions in either systematic theology or exegesis or both. In my opinion, exegesis and systematic theology belong together, in one large-scale project of understanding the Bible better. But in current scholarly practice, the two disciplines have their own distinctive subcultures, so that an analysis of patterns of development and revolution must to some extent treat the disciplines separately.

After changes in theological systems come changes in views on individual points—for example, changes in points of doctrine if one is a systematic theologian, or changes in interpretations of individual texts if one is an exegete. Many of these changes will not seem revolutionary. But many do still involve a kind of change of perspective, in which all the parts get rearranged and are seen in a new way. For instance, consider someone who changes from interpreting the subject of Romans 7:14–25 as a regenerate person to interpreting it as someone who is unregenerate. Such a change involves a simultaneous alternation in one's understanding of nearly all the verses, of the verses' relations to one another, and of the relation of the passage to neighboring passages.

A similar kind of classification has already been suggested in the philosophy of science. After the appearance of the first edition of Kuhn's *Structure of Scientific Revolutions,* Margaret Masterman endeavored to clarify Kuhn's multiple uses of the word *paradigm.*[6] Masterman distinguishes not less than twenty-one different senses. They all refer to clusters of beliefs of one kind or another, but she observes that they fall into three main categories.

In the first, broadest category are "metaphysical paradigms." These are the unquestioned presuppositions about the nature of the world. They are analogous to what we have called world views. A second, narrower category consists in "sociological paradigms," roughly what Kuhn later called disciplinary matrices. These are the specific assumptions and values in the background of a specific discipline. They are analogous to theological systems in systematic theology or hermeneutical systems in exegetical disciplines.

Third, there are "artifact" or "construct" paradigms, what Kuhn later calls exemplars. These are the specific scientific achievements, embodied in crucial theoretical advances and crucial experimental results supporting the theories. This third category is in some ways the most important for Kuhn, and it is also the one that tends to distinguish science from other academic disciplines. Exemplars that have been accepted as

---

[6] Margaret Masterman, "The Nature of a Paradigm," in *Criticism and the Growth of Knowledge,* ed. Imre Lakatos and Alan Musgrave (Cambridge: Cambridge University Press, 1970), pp. 59–90. See also the reflections in Douglas Lee Eckberg and Lester Hill, Jr., "The Paradigm Concept and Sociology: A Critical Review," in *Paradigms and Revolutions: Appraisals and Applications of Thomas Kuhn's Philosophy of Science,* ed. Gary Gutting (Notre Dame: University of Notre Dame Press, 1980), pp. 117–36.

models by an entire community of scientists have a key role in the puzzle-solving process that characterizes normal science.

Biblical interpretation has no exact analogy. Standard theological answers in specific areas of doctrine (such as the ancient creeds provided) and standard exegetical answers on specific texts are similar to exemplars in at least some ways. They are results to which people often refer back. However, they do not usually serve as a model for future research. The creedal formulations with respect to the doctrine of God have for the most part functioned as decisive formulations of a given point of doctrine, not as models of how theology is to be done in other areas. Each area of doctrine needs its own solution, and it is not clear how the solution in one area could serve as a model.

In a very few cases, however, one may find examples that come closer to being exemplars in a Kuhnian sense. Within the historical-critical method, the classic four-document hypothesis about the sources of the Pentateuch became something of an exemplar for how source criticism ought to be done on any book of the Bible. Scholarly work on the Pentateuch was expected to make advances by solving puzzles about particular texts on the basis of the overall framework provided by the four-document hypothesis. The work of Evangelicals was virtually excluded from this scholarly community of historical-critical scholarship in the Old Testament because Evangelicals would not work on the basis of this paradigm. Within the twentieth century, of course, we have seen the paradigm begin to break up under the weight of anomalies.

KNOWLEDGE AS CONTEXTUALLY COLORED

Do all the types of changes considered above really have anything special about them? Why not just talk about changes in people and in their views? Kuhn would not have had anything original to say if he claimed only that science changes with time and that the views of scientists change. What makes Kuhn so interesting, and potentially fruitful, is his claim that knowledge does not always change by piecemeal additions and subtractions. Human knowledge is not to be viewed as so many bits, added to the total sum of knowledge like so many marbles to a pile. Rather, what we know is colored by the framework in which we have our knowledge. This framework includes assumptions, values, procedures, standards, and so on, in the particular field of knowledge.[7]

Even what we see, or what seem to be the most elementary steps in knowledge or data that provide a basis for knowledge, are things seen and already to an extent organized in a way conditioned by our education, background, and experience. Kuhn discusses at some length a psychological experiment with anomalously marked playing cards (e.g., a black seven of hearts or a red three of spades).[8] When allowed to look at a card only for a short time, subjects saw what they thought were normal cards. When longer exposures were used, subjects often became emotionally upset or uneasy without becoming aware of the actual source of their unease. Another experiment with special glasses that inverted the visual field showed that, after a time of adjustment, subjects saw the world normally once again (even though their retinal images were the reverse of normal). Such experiments suggest a much more general principle, already anticipated in Gestalt psychology: understanding a part is influenced by understanding the whole. The influence may be subtle or radical. Knowledge is contextually conditioned.

This contextual conditioning easily explains why it is so notoriously difficult to argue someone into an alternation of the type considered in the previous section. For instance, as is well known, arguments aiming at religious conversion often do not succeed. Failures occur not merely because potential converts have deep emotional investments in religious views that they already hold but because they have difficulty integrating any particular argument offered them into their own full-fledged

---

[7] Kuhn is aware of the potentially radical character of his viewpoint; he speaks of anomalies within the "epistemological viewpoint that has most often guided Western philosophy for three centuries" (Kuhn, *Structure of Scientific Revolutions*, p. 126).

[8] Ibid., pp. 62–64.

framework of knowledge, assumptions, standards, values, and the like. Judged by *their* standards, or by what they suppose that they know, the argument does not seem plausible.

For instance, to the modern materialist, as to the ancient Greek, claims about a resurrection from the dead are ludicrous (Acts 17:32). To the pantheist or animist, claims that the natural world reveals its Creator are missing the point. I do not say that no communication is possible, only that substantive communication takes discipline and patience.[9] One must make explicit the hidden assumptions behind the rejection of the Christian message.

Similarly, arguments between Arminians and Calvinists may easily become ineffective. To someone with an Arminian framework, the Calvinist claim that God decrees all things sounds like fatalism. Passages that appear to teach or imply God's decretal control must be interpreted otherwise, in view of the clear passages about human choice and responsibility on which Arminianism feels itself to be solidly based. Conversely, Arminian appeals to the passages on human responsibility do not move the Calvinist. Since clear passages on divine sovereignty have confirmed the Calvinist position, the passages on human responsibility must be understood as speaking of such responsibility within the framework of divine control. If we cannot resolve the relation of the two in our own mind, it does not mean that such a resolution is impossible for God.

As theological debaters have found out, appeal to a proof text does not always persuade the opponent. From the advocate's point of view, the implications of the proof text seem to be clear. But the opposing position, *as an entire framework for analysis and synthesis,* provides standard resources for handling problem texts.

SEEING PATTERNS

We can illustrate some influences of contextual knowledge even at the level of interpreting an individual text. Let us return

---

[9]See analogous remarks in ibid., pp. 200-204.

again to Romans 7:14–25. Historically, a large part of the debate has centered on two alternatives, the regenerate interpretation and the unregenerate interpretation. Behind this debate lurked an assumption commonly made by both sides, namely, that these two interpretations are the only alternatives. Such an assumption seems natural. Every person is either regenerate or not; hence, the passage must be speaking about one or the other. This assumption, then, functioned as part of the disciplinary matrix for reflection on the meaning of Romans 7:14–25. It was part of the context of knowledge informing the discussion of any details of the passage. Hence to establish one's own alternative, one had only to refute the other alternatives. One can see this pattern in commentaries up to this day. John Murray, for example, lists five main points in favor of the regenerate interpretation.[10] Four out of the five points include a remark to the effect that a given aspect of Romans 7:14–15 is impossible for an unregenerate person. These four points in effect presuppose the assumption that, if Romans 7:14–25 is inconsistent with an unregenerate person, it must be dealing with one who is regenerate.

Consider now the effect of introducing the second-blessing interpretation. This interpretation introduces a third option, and suddenly it is no longer so easy to establish one's own alternative. The alternatives that appeared to cover the field now no longer do. To say that a regenerate person is in view in Romans 7:14–25 is no longer enough. Murray, in fact, notes the existence of a third alternative, but then does not address the possibility that it may be correct.[11] Technically, the third alternative agrees with Murray that the passage considers one who is regenerate. But instead of being the regenerate person in general, it is more specifically a regenerate person who has lapsed from an ideal that is possible in this life. Hence, an argument that beforehand appeared to establish a solid case now reveals some crucial holes.

---

[10]John Murray, *The Epistle to the Romans* (Grand Rapids: Eerdmans, 1959), 1:257–59.

[11]Ibid., 1:257 n. 19.

We can make the situation still more complicated by introducing still another view. According to D. Martin Lloyd-Jones, the person of Romans 7:14–25 is "neither unregenerate nor regenerate."[12] Lloyd-Jones's claim sounds contradictory, but what he actually has in view is perfectly sensible. He refers to "awakened sinners," people who, under the influence of preaching, Bible reading, or other forms of contact with the Christian faith, have come to realize that they are guilty before a holy God. But these people have not yet understood the work of Christ and have not come to an assurance of forgiveness and death to sin. In theory, of course, such people would still be either regenerate or unregenerate in an absolute sense. But when we meet such people, we may not be able to tell which is the case. Moreover, such people do not match what we know of the typical unregenerate or the typical regenerate person.

Now suppose that one returns to Murray's commentary after hearing Lloyd-Jones's position. Murray's arguments, which before appeared solid, now seem dubious. Murray's interpretation may still be right in the end. But his whole argument is going to have to be rethought, because it apparently does not anticipate the possibility of Lloyd-Jones's interpretation. Murray's argument in effect assumes that Romans 7:14–25 cannot be describing personal characteristics intermediate between typical regenerate and typical unregenerate cases.

The alternative interpretations produced by second-blessing theology and by Lloyd-Jones are interesting because of the way in which they break up a previously established pattern of looking at the passage. People using this old pattern could not see that any other alternative was possible.

The second-blessing alternative presents, in a sense, a relatively mild challenge to the pattern. It says, "There indeed are regenerate and unregenerate people. The person spoken of in Romans 7:14–25 must be one or the other. But there may be further subdivisions within these basic types." The arguments

---

[12] D. Martin Lloyd-Jones, *Romans*, 2 vols. (Grand Rapids: Zondervan, 1973), 4:256.

will then no longer proceed the same way in detail. A tension between Romans 7:14–25 and Romans 8, for example, has more than one solution if the former may be describing one type of regenerate person, and Romans 8, another type.

Lloyd-Jones's approach is more radical, because it partly denies the relevance of the regenerate/unregenerate contrast itself. According to Lloyd-Jones, Paul is not asking himself whether the person in question is regenerate or unregenerate. Paul is describing a psychological and spiritual state that cuts across the old categories. Its symptoms are intermediate between the symptoms usually characterizing regenerate people and those characterizing unregenerate people. Lloyd-Jones, one might say, is asking us to focus on a different question altogether. We should not ask, "Are they regenerate or unregenerate?" but, "What spiritual symptoms do they show in response to the law?" Lloyd-Jones has changed the debate by focusing on a cluster of spiritual symptoms rather than on the root of the process, namely whether or not the Holy Spirit has worked regeneration.

For a theologian, it seems so natural to go to the root of the matter immediately and ask about regeneration. Regeneration is the theologically important watershed, and so surely it must be the right question to ask here. To construe theological texts against the background of regeneration is, or was, part of the disciplinary matrix of doing theology.

But Lloyd-Jones did not take this step. Why not? One might wonder whether Lloyd-Jones discovered an alternative partly because of his previous experience in medicine. In medicine, the distinction between symptom and cause is common. Did Lloyd-Jones, then, find it natural to apply this distinction in a new field?[13] Kuhn points out that people coming from another discipline are more likely to make innovative steps.[14] They are not fully assimilated to the reigning disciplinary matrix.

---

[13] Lloyd-Jones's book, *Spiritual Depression: Its Causes and Cure* (Grand Rapids: Eerdmans, 1966), shows signs of the author's medical background.

[14] Kuhn, *Structure of Scientific Revolutions,* p. 90.

Despite Lloyd-Jones's paradoxical language ("neither unregenerate nor regenerate"), his distinction is not really a third category alongside regenerate and unregenerate. Rather, it superimposes another plane of discussion, the plane of spiritual symptoms in response to the law. This tack subtly alters the entire nature of the discussion and the use of Romans 7. Romans is not first of all a theological treatise or a classification; it is a kind of handbook for pastoral care.

People usually do not realize that this kind of shift of viewpoint is possible until they are shown. The whole history of interpretation may miss an important alternative interpretation simply because it includes a framework of assumptions in which some questions are asked (regenerate or unregenerate) and others are not (which symptoms does the spiritual patient show?).

The experience of interpreters of Romans 7 is indeed reminiscent of the psychological experiments with human vision to which Kuhn refers. To some extent, people see what their past experience has trained them to expect to see. The subjects in the psychological experiments, having been trained by experience to see red hearts and black spades, typically do not notice that a different category, a red spade, is before their eyes. They may even become emotionally upset over seeing a red spade. Similarly, interpreters of Romans 7 think only of the categories of regenerate and unregenerate even when other categories are possible in principle. And possibly, like the subjects in the psychological experiments, they become emotionally upset over the controversies that ensue in interpretation.

Some puzzles and riddles also offer suggestive analogies. In one riddle, people are told that Jim's father died in a car accident in which Jim was seriously injured. When Jim arrived at the hospital, the surgeon looked at him and said, "I cannot operate on him, because he is my son." People do not solve the riddle until they question the underlying assumption, based perhaps on generalization from their past experience, that the surgeon is a man, not a woman.

In another puzzle, a gardener is given the assignment of

planting four trees so that each tree is equidistant from each of the other three trees.[15] People do not solve the problem unless they question the assumption that the trees are planted on level ground. The problem can be solved by planting three trees on level ground at the vertices of an equilateral triangle and the fourth tree on a hill in the middle of the triangle.

As a final example, try to connect all nine dots of figure 2 by placing a pencil on one dot, and then drawing four straight lines without once raising the pencil from the paper. People solve the puzzle only when they question the natural (but unjustified) assumption that the line segments are not allowed to extend beyond the outermost dots.

Figure 2. Drawing Puzzle

In general, we may not see a possible solution to a riddle or a puzzle until we abandon a way of thinking that has become a rut. Likewise, in Bible study we may not see a possible interpretive alternative until we abandon familiar ways of thinking.

We are still not through with Romans 7:14–25. Herman Ridderbos advocates still a fifth approach to interpreting the passage.[16] According to Ridderbos, the basic contrast here is

---

[15] This and the following example are taken from Edward de Bono, *Lateral Thinking: Creativity Step by Step* (New York: Harper & Row, 1970), pp. 94–95.

[16] Herman Ridderbos, *Aan de Romeinen* (Kampan: Kok, 1959).

not regenerate versus unregenerate, neither is it a contrast of symptoms of spiritual patients (for example, unawakened vs. awakened vs. at-home-with-Christ). It is the contrast of two ages, pre-Pentecost and post-Pentecost. Prior to the resurrection of Christ and the sending of the Holy Spirit in Pentecostal power and presence, the people of God were bound under the law of Moses. Now they are "released from the law so that [they] serve in the new way of the Spirit, and not in the old way of the written code" (Rom. 7:6).

Paul is not talking here merely about the general fact that God in His holiness passes judgment against everyone who sins, and that in this sense they are under His standards (or "law"). The law is concretely a "written code" (*grammatos,* Rom. 7:6)— the law of Moses. It is the law in its full particularity, including food laws and ceremonial sacrifices. Historically only the Jews, as God's people in special covenant with Him, were under its provisions. And now those who have died with Christ have been released.

Ridderbos introduces another dimension to reading Romans 7. All of the previous interpretations shared a common assumption: that Paul was making statements about the common condition of all people, irrespective of the historical circumstances. All were sinners, all fell short of the glory of God, all were condemned by God's righteous standards, all who were saved were saved by faith in Christ, all were justified by faith and so freed from the curse of God's condemnation, and so on. The preceding set of assumptions is nothing less than the common disciplinary framework of assumptions about Paul, Romans, and the New Testament.

Ridderbos does not disagree with any of the doctrines of this theology as such. But he maintains that here Paul was focusing not just on the biography of individuals standing before God but on the history of the race and of the Jews as the people of God uniquely set apart from all other peoples. Paul was writing about *historia redemptionis* (history of redemption), not simply or primarily about *ordo salutis* (steps in the salvation of an individual).[17]

The categories that Ridderbos uses cut across the conventional categories unregenerate and regenerate. Ridderbos is saying that Paul focuses not on the spiritual state of the individual in abstract terms (unregenerate vs. regenerate), nor on the symptoms of response to the law (unawakened vs. awakened), but on the systematic differences in life created by the objective transition between two orders of existence (under the law of Moses vs. under the realm of union with the resurrected Christ).

It is interesting that people within the same doctrinal tradition can advocate different interpretations of this chapter. Calvin, Lloyd-Jones, and Ridderbos, all adherents of Reformed theology, advocate respectively the regenerate interpretation, the awakened-sinner interpretation, and the pre-Pentecost interpretation of Romans 7:14–25. The differences between them must accordingly be viewed not as differences between systems of theology but as differences affecting only the interpretation of a single passage.

But we should note that the differences are capable of becoming differences of theological style of an extensive kind. Followers of Calvin have traditionally made it a point to read many other passages with the regenerate/unregenerate distinction in mind. Followers of Lloyd-Jones might also read many other passages in terms of the questions of spiritual symptoms. Followers of Ridderbos might make it a policy to read many other passages in terms of the transition of ages between the Old Testament and the New Testament. In fact, Ridderbos participates in the redemptive-historical tradition within New Testament biblical theology that has adopted precisely this emphasis. This tradition claims consistently to arrive at more accurate interpretations of texts within the redemptive-historical framework. The transition to this framework from a preceding framework of reading passages in terms of just-

---

[17] See also the discussion in Douglas J. Moo, "Israel and Paul in Romans 7:7–12," *New Testament Studies* 32 (1986): 122–35.

ification and *ordo salutis* might possibly be analyzed in terms of the categories of revolution.

WHY LIMITED VISION DOES NOT IMPLY RELATIVISM

Some readers may ask whether my analysis above leads to relativism. Does it mean that a text such as Romans 7:14–25 has no fixed meaning but that the meaning depends on the framework (disciplinary matrix) that one uses to look at the text? Does it mean that systems of theology (e.g., Roman Catholicism, Calvinism, or Arminianism) are neither right nor wrong, but all are right depending on the disciplinary matrix one uses in systematic theology? Similar questions were addressed to Kuhn in the wake of his book on revolutions in science.[18]

Kuhn's answer is complex. He is not a nihilist or a relativist in the sense of believing that the choice between systems is irrational. Theists, however, are bound to be dissatisfied with Kuhn's answer, because they do not believe that human beings are the only standard for truth. The proper standard for truth is not found in human beings corporately or individually but in God who is the source of all truth.[19]

Accordingly one must say that there is a right and wrong in the interpretation of Romans 7, and a right and wrong in a theological system. However, it is not necessarily easy for human beings to arrive at what is right. Larger frameworks or disciplinary matrices have an influence. In part, the influence is a good one. An effective, fruitful disciplinary matrix regularly steers researchers toward fruitful ways of looking at a passage and fruitful ways of analyzing and solving theological difficulties. But any disciplinary matrix, by suggesting solutions primarily in one direction, can make people almost blind to the possibility of solutions in another direction. Such, surely, is one of the lessons to draw from the history of interpretation of Romans 7.

---

[18] Kuhn, *Structure of Scientific Revolutions,* pp. 205–7.

[19] On this question, see further my discussion in Poythress, *Symphonic Theology: The Validity of Multiple Perspectives in Theology* (Grand Rapids: Zondervan, 1987).

7

MODELS IN SCIENCE AND IN BIBLICAL INTERPRETATION

We need now to look at one major factor in the disciplinary matrices of natural sciences, namely, the use of models. It is important to consider models because of their influence on what investigators see or fail to see. Models are detailed analogies between one subject and another. The subject needing explanation or visualization is called the "principal" subject, while the one used to do the explaining is called the "subsidiary" subject.[1] In the billiard-ball model of a gas, for example, a gas is represented as a large number of billiard balls moving in all directions through an enclosed space. The gas itself is the principal subject, while the moving billiard balls are the subsidiary subject.

As a second example, consider Newton's theory of gravitation. Newton's equation $F = GmM/r^2$, along with Newton's laws linking force and motion, is a mathematical model for motion in a gravitational field. The mathematical equations are the subsidiary subject, while the moving physical objects are the principal subject.

Models can be of many kinds, depending on the type of

---

[1] The terminology is taken from Max Black, *Models and Metaphors: Studies in Language and Philosophy* (Ithaca: Cornell University Press, 1962), p. 44. Black's book forms one of the principal backgrounds for our discussion.

subsidiary subject chosen and the relations between the subsidiary subject and the principal subject. Thus we may speak of mathematical models, mechanical models, electrical models, scale models, and so on.

INFLUENCE OF MODELS IN SCIENCE

In science models play the role of illustrating theories already considered established. A scale model of the solar system makes the astronomical theory of the solar system clearer to the neophyte. More important, models play an important role in the discovery and improvement of new scientific theories. The billiard-ball model of a gas was crucial to the development of the kinetic theory of gases and its predictions about gas pressure, temperature, and the like. Similarly, James Clerk Maxwell developed his theory of electricity and magnetism by creative use of analogy between electricity (principal subject) and an ideal incompressible fluid (subsidiary subject). Today physicists would be likely to say that Maxwell's equations are the real model (a mathematical model) and that we can dispense with the fluid. But in Maxwell's own day people were still thinking in terms of an ether that was a real physical object and that might have properties analogous to a fluid.[2]

A properly chosen analogy thus suggests questions to be asked, lines of research, or possible general laws. Mathematical equations known to hold for the subsidiary subject can be carried over to the principal subject, albeit sometimes with slight modifications. The analogy needs to be used flexibly, because the principal subject is usually not analogous to the subsidiary subject in all respects.[3]

Everyone agrees that models have a decisive role in *discovery*. But what happens after the theory is drawn up? Philosophy of science in the positivist tradition would like to say that models are dispensable when it comes to assessing the

---

[2] Ibid., pp. 226–28.
[3] See Maxwell's discussion, quoted in ibid., p. 226.

justification of theories and their truth content. Others, Max Black included, think that some models are an integral, indissoluble part of the finished theory.[4] Even a mathematical model consists not merely in a mathematical formula but also in rules of thumb for relating the mathematics to the phenomena. These rules of thumb cannot be completely formalized without losing some of the potential of the model to suggest extensions to other phenomena. Thomas Kuhn does not address directly this question about models in *The Structure of Scientific Revolutions*. But from what he says about the role of exemplars and disciplinary matrices in directing further lines of research, one can infer that he agrees with Black about the indispensability of models.

Is biblical interpretation analogous to science in its use of models? To be sure, some models are to be found within the Bible itself. Adam, for example, is a model for Christ with respect to his role in representing humanity (Rom. 5:12–21). But analogies in biblical interpretation seldom have the detailed, quantitative character of mathematical models or physical models in science. Perhaps we had better talk about analogies rather than models.[5]

Now let us ask whether models (analogies) are dispensable in biblical interpretation. Even if we granted that in theory they were dispensable in natural science, it would be difficult to present an analogous argument for biblical interpretation. The less-than-exact character of models in biblical interpretation means that they are most often not dispensable.

As an example, take again Romans 5:12–21. Can we eliminate the comparison with Adam and still retain the

---

[4] See ibid., pp. 219–43.

[5] For a further exploration of the use of models, analogies, and metaphors, see Ian Barbour, *Myths, Models, and Paradigms: A Comparative Study in Science and Religion* (New York: Harper & Row, 1974); and Sallie McFague TeSelle, *Speaking in Parables: A Study in Metaphor and Theology* (Philadelphia: Fortress, 1975). Barbour and TeSelle presuppose a non-Evangelical view of biblical authority. Evangelicals will find in their works a combination of stimulating insights and the effort to displace biblical teaching by analogically projecting biblical language into the framework of modern culture.

theological substance of the passage? We could, to be sure, paraphrase a good deal of the main points in order to eliminate specific reference to Adam. But even if we studied such a paraphrase for a long time, we would miss something. Romans 5:12–21 has a suggestiveness about it that is characteristic of metaphor.[6] It invites us to think of many ways in which Adam and Christ are analogous (and dissimilar). Once we eliminate completely any reference to Adam, we thereby eliminate the possibility of exploring just how far these analogies extend.

ANALOGY IN ROMANS 7

Do analogies really make a difference in interpretive controversies? Sometimes, at least, they do. Ridderbos, for example, argues that Romans 7 has in view primarily the contrast between two ages, before and after the resurrection of Christ and the day of Pentecost. Romans 7:14–25, we might say, is analogous to the statements elsewhere in Scripture about the resurrection of Christ, the coming of the kingdom of God, and the fulfillment of the ages. The model that Ridderbos assumes is the model of two ages and a redemptive transition between them. By contrast, the model that the regenerate and the unregenerate interpretations assume is the model of the individual soul and its life. Using such a model, Romans 7:14–25 is viewed as analogous to the statements about individual experiences of being saved.

These two models are not tight-knit and mathematically describable structures like models in natural science. They are more like generalizations or clusters of patterns derived from a loose collection of biblical texts. Ridderbos shows us common patterns linking much of what Paul (and other New Testament writers) say about the death of Christ, the resurrection of Christ, the coming of the Spirit, the reconciliation of Jews and Gentiles, and events representing a global transition of redemptive epochs. Against this background he invites us to see Romans 7:14–25 as an embodiment of the pattern. Likewise the

---

[6] See Black, *Models and Metaphors*, pp. 38–47.

regenerate interpretation collects verses describing the situation of individuals who are Christian and who are not Christian and invites us to see the same passage as embodying a pattern corresponding to the passages that describe Christians.

Both of these models do not so much exploit a particular analogy (say, with the resurrection of Christ or with the conversion of Cornelius) as they use generalized patterns. They are less like a metaphor than like a generalization. Moreover, to a large extent these models describe what we may bring to any text whatsoever when we study it.

But we may also ask whether a particular text introduces its own analogies. For example, Romans 7:2–4 clearly invokes an analogy using marriage as the subsidiary subject, in order to elucidate a principal subject, namely, our responsibilities toward the law and toward Christ. What analogies, then, are operative in verses 7–25? It is difficult to decide whether there is any dominant analogy. But when interpreters come to the passage, they may have an analogical framework in which they understand biblical descriptions of sin. In the Bible as a whole there are a number of basic analogies or metaphors for explaining, illustrating, and driving home to readers the power of sin.

First, sin is viewed as a sickness. Using this analogy, one can emphasize the power of sin by arguing that this sickness has infected every part of the body (e.g., Isa. 1:5–6; James 3:8). Second, sin is like darkness. One can stress sin's power by pointing out that every part of people is dark (e.g., Eph. 4:18; Luke 11:33–36). Third, sin is like fire. One points out the power of sin by affirming that it is unstoppable (James 3:6). Finally, sin is like the relationship of a master to a slave. In this analogy, one points out the power of sin by showing that, however the slave may struggle to become free, the master will subdue him. Romans 6 uses this analogy in describing the situation before having died with Christ.

Which analogies are operating in Romans 7:14–25? If we have the analogy with sickness or darkness, we expect to find affirmations about the pervasiveness of sickness or darkness in the unregenerate. What is actually said in the passage appears to be inconsistent with such a pervasive sickness. Hence the regenerate interpretation appears to be more attractive. On the other hand, if the analogy is with master and slave (as it appears to be in v. 14), the struggles of the enslaved person to become free may have been introduced to make the point about sin's power more effectively. Hence the mention of the struggles of the "mind" in verse 23 might still be compatible with the unregenerate interpretation. When we use this perspective the unregenerate interpretation appears more attractive, inasmuch as similar points about sin's mastery over the unregenerate are made in Romans 6. One's preference for the regenerate or unregenerate interpretation (or still some other interpretation) may therefore be influenced by what one sees as the governing analogy here.

Perhaps, however, the problem is still deeper. Do we come to Scripture expecting to find a single, uniform theory of sin, accompanied by a single, fixed, precise vocabulary to designate the various states of sin and righteousness? If so, we are predisposed to see difficulties in harmonizing Romans 7:22–23 with statements elsewhere about unregenerate people. Hence the regenerate interpretation wins our allegiance.

Suppose, however, that we approach Scripture expecting to find a number of analogies making complementary points. Since each analogy is partial, the various analogies may sometimes superficially appear to be at odds with one another. For example, the analogy with slavery may appear to be at odds with the analogy of sickness. In the slavery analogy, the slave may attempt rebellion only to illustrate how inescapable is the master's dominion. But the slave's rebellious activity appears to contradict what the sickness analogy says about the pervasive penetration of the disease. We reconcile the two only by recognizing that each is a partial analogy about the nature of sin. Using this approach, we are then able to harmonize the unregenerate interpretation of Romans 7:22–23, which uses a slave analogy, with the texts elsewhere in Paul using the analogy of sickness or darkness.

We may extend our example in another direction. Our reading of Romans 7:14–25 depends on the kind of exposition of sin that we expect. Do we anticipate a colorful, imaginative, dramatic characterization? Then sin can be personified as the master, the individual as the slave, and the subsequent imaginary confrontation traced out. Or do we expect a careful, scientific exposition analyzing the ontological relations of the various human faculties, as these are touched by sin? In the latter case we are predisposed to find verses 22–23 consistent only with what is said of the regenerate mind, because words like *mind* and *flesh* must always designate the same fixed aspects of human beings. In the former case, we are predisposed to allow that these two verses might simply be making a different point by dramatization. Hence even if these verses referred to an unregenerate person, it would not contradict the point made elsewhere when the unregenerate are characterized as dead and unresponsive to God.

A ROLE FOR ANALOGY IN THEOLOGICAL CONTROVERSIES

What difference does it make that biblical interpretation employs analogies? First, some people could say that this leads to the conclusion that biblical interpretation and, with its resulting theology, is "mere" analogy, hence not really true to the facts, and that knowing objective truth is impossible.

But such a conclusion misunderstands the power of analogy. Analogies at their best are aids to the truth rather than hindrances. Remember that sciences use analogies in the form of models, and the Bible itself uses analogies. We need to say that, when we read a passage of the Bible, the analogies or models that we have in mind influence what we see and influence our judgments about which competing interpretations are plausible. Becoming aware of some of the analogies that we are using and some of the alternatives that might be possible may help us to understand the Bible better.

For example, in interpreting Romans 7, is it better to be aware of the several alternative approaches? Knowing that there are several alternatives could wrongly make us think, "There is no right answer. Any answer is O.K., because any answer can be achieved if we start with the right analogy."

But I would disagree. One answer is right. Of course, there can be overlapping partial answers, more than one of which could be right as far as it goes. But the major alternatives in interpreting Romans 7 are mutually exclusive, unless we claim that Paul was intentionally ambiguous (which is not plausible here). Hence one of the alternatives is right. But we can properly judge the relative claims of the alternatives only when we view each one of them in its strongest form and compare it with the others. As long as we are unaware of the possibility of using an alternate analogy (one that Paul himself may have had in mind in writing), we are not in as good a position to make an accurate judgment.

The same holds true when we consider theological doctrines or theological systems rather than individual passages of the Bible. Consider, for example, the doctrinal dispute between creationism and traducianism. Creationism says that God, by an immediate act, creates the soul of each new human being who comes into the world. On the other hand, according to traducianism, the soul of the child derives by providential processes from the soul of the parents.

Each of these two views appeals to various biblical passages. Each passage must be studied and weighed in its own right. We can never eliminate this step in theology. But we should also be aware that each view is made plausible partly by the use of a governing analogy. For traducianism, the key analogy is between generation of the soul and generation of the body. After the initial direct creation of Adam in Genesis 1–2, the propagation of the race takes place by providence. The bodies of children are formed providentially from substance deriving from their parents. The traducianist claims that the generation of the soul is analogous. In addition, a realist view of human nature sometimes enters into traducianism, and such realism rests on an analogy between human souls and parts of a whole. The souls are related to human nature as parts are to a whole.

For creationism, on the other hand, the principal analogy is between the generation of the soul and the creative acts of God in Genesis, which create new beings. Both of these acts of making new things contrast with the later providential acts of God, in which He sustains what He has already made.

Being aware of these analogies does not by itself tell us which of these two positions is right. (Or perhaps some combination of the two or a third alternative could be right.) But such awareness can alert us to some of the reasons why both positions are attractive and why both have had their advocates.

Next, consider classic dispensationalism and classic covenant theology as examples of theological systems. Each system gives an important role to a certain key concept. For covenant theology, that concept is the covenant of grace; for dispensationalism, it is the dispensations, that is, epochs marked by distinctive arrangements in God's government of human beings. Covenant theology naturally leads to a concentration on the salvific purposes of God. Such purposes are embodied in the covenant of grace and form a main strand to which other purposes of God are linked. Dispensationalism, on the other hand, has classically been interested in the purpose that the dispensations serve by showing success or failure of human beings under different governmental arrangements. Salvation of individuals runs alongside this purpose.

Dispensationalism and covenant theology are both complex systems. They cannot simply be reduced to some one analogy. And yet analogy has an important role. In covenant theology, the covenant of grace is understood as embodied in (and therefore analogous to) the concrete covenants mentioned in the Bible, which in turn are analogous to treaties or contracts made between human beings (except that God sovereignly lays down the conditions). In dispensationalism, the governing analogy in understanding dispensations is the analogy between God the great King and a human ruler who inaugurates a new form of government.

TYPES OF ANALOGIES

We have already uncovered a considerable diversity of analogies used in biblical interpretation, many of which occur in the Bible itself. Here we may distinguish six distinct uses of analogy.

First, a one-line comparison, a small-scale analogy, in the form of a simple metaphor or simile. For example, Psalm 23:5, "You prepare a table before me in the presence of my enemies," compares God's provision with that of a host.

Second, an extended analogy, constituting a controlling force in a whole passage. Most of the parables of Jesus (the parable of the lost sheep, the parable of the great banquet, the parable of the mustard seed, the parable of the wheat and the tares, and so on) use an analogy in this way. But analogies can also be used in direct exposition of theological truths. For example, analogies with dying and slavery control the extended discussion in Romans 6. The analogy between Adam and Christ controls Romans 5:12–21. Sometimes the use of an analogy may be more subtle than in these instances. For example, the interpretation of Romans 7:14–25 partly turns on the question of whether Paul is here using a sort of dramatic, theatrical analogy between sin and a human being, on the one hand, and two personal opponents striving with one another for mastery, on the other. Because Paul does not say, in so many words, "Now let us compare one thing to another," it is more difficult to assess what he is doing.

Third, an analogy used repeatedly in different passages in the Bible, so that it constitutes a biblical theme. For example, comparisons of God with a king or a father frequently form a biblical theme, as do comparisons between God's relations to human beings and agreements, or covenants, between human beings.

Fourth, an analogy used to help interpret a passage, even though it is not the governing analogy for the passage itself. For example, in discussing Romans 7, if we wanted to defend a dramatic understanding of what Paul is doing, we might appeal not only to an analogy with drama in general but also to an analogy with other passages of the Bible that present moral conflict in more dramatic terms: for example, the personifications of wisdom and folly in Proverbs 7–9. Neither drama in general nor Proverbs 7–9 in particular is a governing force in the actual structure of Romans 7. Both of these analogies, however, might make it easier for someone to see that Paul perhaps is speaking in a more dramatically colored, semipersonified way about sin in its relation to human beings.

Fifth, an analogy used in formulating a particular doctrine. For example, the analogy between generation of the soul and generation of the body is used by traducianism.

Sixth, an analogy used as a key element in a theological or hermeneutical system. For example, the covenant of grace, analogous to covenants between human beings, is a key element in classic covenant theology.

To a certain extent, these different types of analogies are related to the different types of disciplinary matrices that were discussed in chapter 6. Just as in science, so also in biblical interpretation, a disciplinary matrix within a given field is likely to make use of some controlling analogy. Some analogies function as master analogies and thus control a larger field. The idea of covenant, for example, analogous to human treaties or agreements, influences the whole system of covenant theology. Other analogies function as useful analogies only within the smaller area of a single doctrine or of the interpretation of a single text.

We should note, however, a certain uniqueness to the largest disciplinary matrix or context for biblical interpretation. As I argued in chapter 6, the deepest factor influencing biblical interpretation is the work of the Holy Spirit in regeneration. Without this work of the Spirit, a person cannot understand what the Spirit teaches in Scripture (1Cor. 2:6–16). This work of the Spirit affects the heart and mind of people in the deepest and fullest way. We cannot fully describe the Spirit's work by saying, for instance, that regeneration is merely making available to a person in an intellectual way some new analogy. Doubtless the Holy Spirit enables the person involved to see the relevance of certain relations and analogies, not only analogies in the Bible itself, but relations between the biblical teaching and the person's own life and experience. But it would be false to say that the work of the Holy Spirit is exhausted in making clear any one analogy. Nor could we say that an unregenerate person would in principle be unable to use a particular analogy. The use of particular analogies is a salient characteristic of less comprehensive disciplinary matrices, but regeneration has a more comprehensive character.

8

ANALOGIES AS PERSPECTIVES

At any one point in our study of the Bible, must we use only one analogy or one type of analogy? To answer this question, let us first look at the situation in natural sciences.

ANALOGIES AS COMPLEMENTARY

In science we are accustomed to seeing one model used as the key element in a particular theory. Other proposed models are discarded when one model gains dominance. For example, the Ptolemaic model, with the earth at the center of the solar system, was discarded after the Copernican model, with the sun at the center, gained dominance. If biblical interpretation is analogous to science at this point, we should expect that the currently favored interpretation would supersede all previous interpretations and would invoke one dominant model.

To some extent, the use of a single dominant model has indeed characterized some theological controversies. The historical-critical method, for example, used as its main analogy the example of historical investigation of secular history. The Bible had to be treated like any other book from the ancient past. This model virtually defined the historical-critical method and gradually gained dominance in academic circles. In these

circles the older "dogmatic" methods of interpretation ceased to
be practiced.

Consider further the controversy between traducianism
and creationism. One of the issues at stake here is the
dominance of an analogy. What is the best analogy for
understanding the origin of individual souls—the analogy with
the generation and growth of the bodies of children or the
analogy with the original creation of new beings in Genesis 1?
Once one decides which analogy is correct, the other analogy is
seen to be invalid and is therefore discarded.

However, this second example gives us pause. On an issue
like traducianism and creationism, it seems that the debate is
difficult to decide, even when we have basic agreement on the
authority of the Bible. Could it be that neither position is
wholly right? Could more than one analogy sometimes apply
(at least up to a point)? At the same time, perhaps no one
analogy captures with superior clarity all the features of biblical
teaching on the subject. The origin of human souls might be
like an original creation in some respects and like the generation
of human bodies in other respects. Then each side would be able
to appeal to verses that appear to validate its position.

In many cases of interpretive controversy, only one
position can be right. In understanding Romans 7, the two
major interpretations, regenerate and unregenerate, cannot both
be right. Perhaps one of the two is right; or perhaps neither is
right, and some third position, like Lloyd-Jones's "awakened
sinner" interpretation, is correct. In the interpretation of
1 Thessalonians 4:4, "one's own vessel" must mean either
"one's own body" or "one's own wife," not both. Likewise,
with respect to the historical-critical revolution, it was either
right or wrong to practice historical reconstruction with
antisupernaturalist assumptions built into the use of historical
analogy.[1]

---

[1] The choice between the historical-critical method and alternative methods is
not always as clear-cut as it may seem. Acknowledgment of the supernatural
can be used as a platform for denying God's involvement with the ordinary, or
for presupposing that God could not use ordinary means in writing Scripture
(such as Luke's research, alluded to in Luke 1:3), or as an excuse to ignore the

In other cases, however, the use of multiple analogies may be permissible. Certainly, the Bible itself uses multiple analogies in its teaching about the church. The church is the temple of God, the body of Christ, and the assembly of God's people (analogous to the assembly of Israelites at Mount Sinai or Mount Zion). These affirmations about the church are complementary rather than contradictory. Similarly, God is a king, a father, and a husband, three analogies expressing complementary truths.

Likewise, we might say that the four Gospels present us with complementary pictures of the earthly life of Christ. Of course, the Gospels do have much in common. The differences among them can easily be exaggerated. Yet, differences of a subtle kind do exist. Such differences are complex and difficult to summarize adequately. Some of the differences of emphasis among the Gospels can indeed be related to differences of perspective on the idea of messiahship. Matthew, for example, strongly emphasizes Christ's Davidic kingship. The Gospel of Matthew begins with a genealogy that includes a list of Davidic kings. John, on the other hand, emphasizes Christ's role as the Son of God. Christ as Son exists in close relation to the Father and reveals the Father in His work. Likewise Mark and Luke have some distinctive emphases.

Christ's messiahship and His work of redemption are so rich in significance that they might be viewed from many angles and in the light of many connections with Old Testament promises and institutions. No one of these approaches by itself would capture everything. Surely the idea of Christ as Davidic King (Matthew) and the idea of Christ as Son revealing the Father (John) are both true. But it would be unfortunate if we used only one of these approaches.

The two ways of explaining Christ and His work invite us to relate His life to two different sets of Old Testament texts. If

human authors and circumstances that God has used in bringing the books of the Bible into being. The historical-critical method, in spite of its bad presuppositions, has sometimes been instrumental in causing reluctant supernaturalists to look at the Bible from angles other than those they would most comfortably adopt on their own initiative.

we say that Christ is Davidic King, we link up our thinking right away with the history of Old Testament kingship, with its successes and failures and with the promises made to David, which never find a final fulfillment within the pages of the Old Testament. If we say that Christ is the Son of God, we make some contact with the texts that speak of Israel as son in a subordinate sense (e.g., Exod. 4:22–23; Deut. 8:5). Christ was obedient to God, whereas Israel failed. We also relate to the Old Testament theme of revelation, both in creation (John 1:1–5) and in redemption (vv. 14, 17).

Furthermore, the two ways of understanding Christ have different purposes apologetically. The emphasis on Davidic kingship corresponds to the interest of Jews in expecting a Davidic Messiah. The emphasis on revelation of the Father proclaims the universal relevance of Christ's work and answers questions about knowing God.

USING MULTIPLE ANALOGIES

We can now generalize this pattern of multiple analogies. In many areas of studying the Bible, it is illuminating and profitable to approach the same text or the same topic from a number of different perspectives, each of which will use a somewhat different analogy or controlling concept.[2] As our test case, let us use 1 Corinthians 3:10–17.

It might seem at first that, in studying this passage, we are confined to using the analogy between believers and a temple. After all, this analogy is the one that Paul himself uses! Anyone who neglects this analogy and substitutes another is just going to ignore or distort what the Bible is saying at this point. Certainly the use of multiple analogies must never overrun or obscure the fact that a single passage often uses a single dominant analogy.

But even in a passage with a clearly dominant analogy, something may be learned from using other analogies. By using other analogies, we obtain illumination, not so much about the

---

[2]For further discussion, see my book *Symphonic Theology*.

passage in itself, but about the relation of the passage to larger concerns in the Bible.

For example, consider the analogy between God and a judge. When this alternate analogy is invoked in the Bible, it teaches at least some of the same things that 1 Corinthians 3:10–17 teaches in its analogy with a temple. For instance, Paul brings in the theme of judgment, particularly in verses 13–15. Consistent with the temple analogy, he speaks of a fire's coming to destroy everything in the building that is made out of poor material. This fire results in a kind of judgment on the building.

The analogy of a judge makes a similar point. God is the Judge, and we as human beings come before Him to have our deeds evaluated. God rewards patience (James 5:7–11) and good labor (2 Cor. 5:10) and punishes evil.

So far, we see that the same things can be said using either analogy. But in addition, the analogy with judging helps to illuminate 1 Corinthians 3:13–15. If we just had verses 10–17 in isolation, we might wonder why there should be a fire at all. Why does it come? Does it have to come? Why should the whole building be encompassed (rather than some people's parts of the building escaping completely)? Observing fires and buildings on earth does not really help us answer these questions. On the other hand, the analogy involving judges clears things up immediately. The fire is there to accomplish the negative judgment on what is inadequate.

Moreover, the analogy with judging also helps us with the question, What is the standard for success or failure? In 1 Corinthians 3:10–17, Paul says that those who build with gold, silver, and precious stones succeed, while those who build with wood, hay, and straw ultimately fail. But what sort of contrast is Paul making? What do gold, silver, and precious stones stand for? That is, what are they analogous to? The mere fact of analogy between temple and group of believers does not make it clear. Paul gives some of the answer in verse 11, where he indicates what the right foundation is. We might guess that the gold, silver, and precious stones represent any activity based on Christ's work. But then verse 12 seems to envision that one might build on this (correct) foundation, but still with the wrong materials. One might guess that using the wrong materials amounts to building in a way inconsistent doctrinally or practically with the foundation, namely, the core of Christianity, the doctrines of Christ. But how would this error differ from not building on the right foundation at all?

To some questions of this kind, Paul may not have given us full answers. The context of discussion about Apollos (1 Cor. 3:4–9) and Peter (1:12) does make it clear that Paul is concerned that teachers should build up unity and that those who follow them should guard that unity. But beyond these conclusions it is hard to be specific.

The analogy with judging can help here. If God is Judge, the standards for judgment will be God's standards. These standards include the concerns for church unity and consistency with the doctrine of Christ (and other things besides). These standards help us to draw out the broader implications of the picture offered in 1 Corinthians 3:10–17. It has a lesson about good workmanship in the church. The lesson certainly applies most immediately to the circumstances of disunity at Corinth. But it will also apply quite broadly to whatever work we do, as measured by all the standards of God's Word.

On the other hand, we must not claim that the analogy with judging is so good that it ought to replace the analogy with the temple. The analogy with a temple is very effective in certain respects. In particular, it shows that defective work in the context of the church receives a reward that is really fitting for it ("If you are foolish enough to build with inferior stuff, anybody can see that you will lose, because the inferior stuff will perish"). This point is less obvious if we use the analogy with judging. Human judges may or may not have good standards of judgment. There may or may not be a connection between the intrinsic quality of one's work and the reward that one gets from the judge. God, of course, is a just judge, so it is different with Him. But an analogy with the temple can help to demonstrate precisely that point.

Now let us use still another analogy, the one between the church and a human body with its members. This analogy is used overtly in 1 Corinthians 12 and Romans 12:4–5. But can we apply this analogy to 1 Corinthians 3:10–17?

Once again, we find a basic harmony. Using the analogy with the temple, 1 Corinthians 3:10–17 makes some of the same basic theological points as those that come out in 1 Corinthians 12 and Romans 12:4–5, which use the analogy with a human body. All three passages are concerned with Christian unity. First Corinthians 3:10–17 makes the point by stressing that all the building must take place on the one foundation. The other two passages make the point by showing that each person in the church has a need for the gifts and contributions of all the other people. Only by working together as many members can there be a healthy, well-functioning body.

But there are also some differences of focus between the passages. First Corinthians 3:10–17, by using an analogy with a fixed structure, helps us to focus on the significance of the once-for-all unity founded in the work of Jesus Christ. Everything that we do in the church must rest on that finished achievement. First Corinthians 12 and Romans 12, on the other hand, focus more on the practical, working, functional unity of the church. It is fitting for them to use the analogy with the human body, since the organs of the body show their unity by practically functioning together toward harmonious goals.

The analogy with the human body can now help to reveal something that otherwise might be mysterious or overlooked in 1 Corinthians 3:10–17. Paul wants the principles of unity and sound growth to be applied not only to the area of teaching content but also to the practical manner in which believers relate to one another (with jealousy, pride, or party spirit, or with humility and gentleness). We might make the mistake of interpreting the fixed, stony character of the pieces of the building in this passage to mean that only doctrinal issues or issues of individual morality were at stake. In view of the rest of 1 Corinthians, such a conclusion would be a mistake.

When we transform 1 Corinthians 3:10–17 into the alternative analogy with the body, we help to make the implications clear. For example, unity on one foundation corresponds to unity in being a member of the body—not just any body, but the body of Christ. Building on the foundation corresponds to functioning as a member of the body. The type of building material corresponds to the type of activity of the member, helpful or unhelpful to the health and goals of the body as a whole. At this point we find the strength of the analogy with the human body. When we use the analogy of the body, we make clear the dependence of each member on the others.

The testing of the building with fire corresponds to the testing on the basis of the history of healthfulness and helpfulness of each member of the body. Here the analogy with the body does not serve us as well as the analogy of judge or some other analogy.

What do we conclude from our analysis of 1 Corinthians 3:10–17? The principles of multiple analogies that we have applied here can be useful with many other texts. When a passage of the Bible is dominated by a single analogy, it is important to take this feature into account and not to pretend that all analogies are equal. But even in such a situation, some details of the passage, or more often aspects of the relation of the passage to its larger context, can be illumined when we use alternate analogies. The alternate analogies may not be absolutely necessary, but they help to draw our attention to aspects of the passage that might otherwise be neglected.

The same lesson holds on a higher level. Consider the general issue of organizing a biblical theology of one or both Testaments. There has been considerable controversy over what is the best organizing theme or center when writing a theology of the Old Testament or of the New Testament. Biblical theology desires to have a center that will capture the inner structure of the biblical material itself, not simply organize the teaching of the Bible in terms of traditional topics (God, human beings, Christ, salvation, last things, etc.).

More than one center has been advocated for the Old Testament: the covenant, the kingdom of God, Israel's confession, and promise.[3] Similarly, for the New Testament there has

---

[3] Gerhard F. Hasel, *Old Testament Theology: Basic Issues in the Current Debate*, rev. ed. (Grand Rapids: Eerdmans, 1972), pp. 77–103.

been debate over two major centers: justification and redemptive history. Should the primary center be the nature of humanity as lost and saved, particularly the work of justification? Or should we have as a center the theme of redemptive history and the transition between epochs of redemption (two ages) achieved in the work of Christ, especially His resurrection?[4]

These issues are complex, and it would be impossible for us to analyze them in detail here. But our argument thus far suggests at least two implications. First, the kind of organizing center chosen does make a difference. It functions as an exemplar, an important element in the disciplinary framework for studying the Bible. To shift from one such center to another may involve a major, even a traumatic, change.

Second, no single organizing center is uniquely the right one. Gerhard F. Hasel, in his books surveying biblical theology of the two Testaments, suggests as much.[5] He wonders whether the Bible is so rich that no one center will succeed in capturing all its aspects equally. In our own framework, we might say that, even if one or more than one center could achieve such a result, there would still be need on a practical level for a variety of analogies and perspectives on the Bible. The Bible itself offers us a variety of analogies in various areas of doctrine. When we attempt to synthesize biblical teaching as a whole, we are bound to try to relate these analogies to one another. The best results would be achieved if these analogies could all illuminate one another. We would then notice aspects of biblical teaching that we might overlook using a single perspective, however correct it might be.

CAN AN ANALOGY REPRESENT TRUTH?

For many modern people, the word *analogy* or *metaphor* tends to suggest something unreal or untrue, a mere rhetorical

---

[4]Gerhard F. Hasel, *New Testament Theology: Basic Issues in the Current Debate* (Grand Rapids: Eerdmans, 1978), pp. 140–70; Herman Ridderbos, *Paul: An Outline of His Theology* (Grand Rapids: Eerdmans, 1975), pp. 13–43.

[5]Hasel, *New Testament Theology*, p. 164; idem, *Old Testament Theology*, p. 141.

trick. Hence it seems to depreciate the seriousness of biblical revelation when we say that the Bible uses many analogies and metaphors and that we should do so too.

However, we must not underestimate the power of metaphors to express truth. Well-chosen metaphors assert the existence of analogies that God has placed in the world, not merely analogies that we impose on an unformed or chaotic world. Thus metaphors assert truth about an analogical structure in the world, and by invoking such analogical structures, they also assert truth about their principal subject. For example, when Paul says, "You yourselves are God's temple" (1 Cor. 3:16), he implies that God Himself has ordained that there would be revealing analogies between temples of stone and the structure of the New Testament community. Both are dwelling places of God, both are holy and involve penalties on those who defile them (v. 17), both have foundations that function to establish a unified plan for the whole, and both are constructed with good or bad workmanship, as the case may be. In implying these things, Paul thereby also implies some true assertions about the nature of his principal subject, the Corinthian church.

Similarly, much of the Bible's language about God Himself is metaphoric in character (so-called anthropomorphic language), but not less true for that reason. The Bible's use of metaphor is both true and useful and functions rightly when we freely recognize such use.

In addition, when biblical metaphors touch on the deepest realities, they often surpass what we would casually expect from a superficial analogy. We can illustrate this principle from 1 Corinthians 3:16. A metaphor invokes an analogy between a principal subject (in this case, the church) and a subsidiary subject (temples). Here the temple is the known original thing, and the church is compared to it. Thus we might say that the temple is the original, while the church is only a copy analogous to this original.[6]

---

[6] In 1 Corinthians 3:10–17, did Paul have in mind a pagan temple or the Jewish temple as his model? Since his metaphor applies to either kind of temple,

But what is a temple? A temple of stone is more than just an architectural object. It symbolically represents religious truth. It is a dwelling place for God (or in the pagan case, for a false god). In fact, temples in the ancient Near East were built somewhat like royal residences. In their architectural arrangements temples themselves exploit a further analogy between God (or gods) and human kings. Whether we look at the temple as a dwelling for God or a residence of a king, the fundamental religious ideas do not depend on there being a stone structure. Something else might serve as a temple as well, for instance, a human body.

In fact, the final temple of God is Christ's body (John 2:20–21). The tabernacle and the temple in the Old Testament were constructed according to God's plan to display beforehand some of the things that would be realized in full only when Christ came (Heb. 8–10). The design of the temple looked forward to Christ, though this fact was not perfectly understood until New Testament times.

It appears, then, that the Old Testament temple was built after analogy with the "real" temple, Christ's human body. Believers in Christ become human temples, not merely temples of stone. In this respect, they are better or more perfect temples than the Old Testament temple of stone and wood. Earlier, at a more superficial level, we said that the stone temple was the original and the church was the copy. Now at a deeper level we find that the church is closer to the original and the stone temple is the copy.

From these observations we may conclude that the church is indeed analogous to the Old Testament temple of stone. Such a statement expresses truth, not illusion. Moreover, the analogy is not an accident. In this case and in many others in the Bible, the analogy reveals a depth dimension that transcends merely

perhaps the question is unnecessary. If we are forced to decide, the Jewish temple is clearly more appropriate to verse 16. There was a vast difference between a pagan temple, which falsely claimed to be a dwelling place of a god, and the Jewish temple, which really was a dwelling place for the true God. Paul says that believers are a real temple for the real God, not a pseudotemple for a pseudogod.

superficial comparisons. We find here multiple relationships based on the profound unity of God's wisdom for creation and redemption. The symbolic structures and institutions of the Old Testament, which seem to be the starting point for forming analogies, are themselves always based on an original in heaven, in the plan of God.

Another example may help make this point clear. When the Bible says that God is king, it uses an analogy between God and human, earthly kings. We would be tempted to say, therefore, that the earthly kings are real kings, whereas God is king only in a secondary, analogical, metaphorical sense. But where do earthly kings come from? God created human beings with power to govern, and God providentially appoints some to be in positions of authority (Ps. 75:6–7; Dan. 2:21; Rom. 13:1–7). In such positions these people are representatives of God and God's authority. Hence human kingship and rule ultimately derive from the fact that God created human beings in His image and that He delegates His kingly power in a limited form to governmental authorities. The earthly kings are not the "real" ones but are kings only in a secondary sense by analogy with the real King, God Himself. Rather than saying that God is described anthropomorphically, we might better say that human beings are described theomorphically, after analogy with God the Original.[7]

In sum, when we identify a biblical saying as an analogy or a metaphor, we should remember that, far from being rhetorical tricks, biblical analogies express profound truths.

FOUNDATIONS FOR MULTIPLICITY IN BIBLICAL INTERPRETATION

One disturbing aspect of using multiple themes or multiple analogies in studying the Bible is that this procedure does not agree with the practice in natural sciences. Once a scientific field has reached a certain stage of maturity, according

---

[7] In using this language, I am indebted to an unpublished comment by James I. Packer.

to Kuhn, it will normally operate in terms of one dominant disciplinary framework. Included in this framework will normally be some specific theories using models. Only in times of revolution, when the existing framework does not seem to be solving problems satisfactorily, will there be some degree of multiplication of analogies or models, as people cast about for some better way of coping. Should biblical interpretation try to imitate science at this point and use only one dominant model or analogy?

There are at least three possible responses to this difficulty. First, we may say that, in biblical interpretation as well as science, the use of multiple analogies or perspectives to describe the same subject is an imperfection that ought to be overcome by the development and consistent use of a single more comprehensive model. Second, we may agree that using multiple perspectives is appropriate in biblical interpretation, but only because biblical interpretation is not really analogous to science. The third response is to say that even within science, it may be too rigid to require a single dominant model.

Let us examine each of these alternatives. First, should biblical interpretation strive ideally to use only a single dominant model? Scientific practice shows us that scientists usually pursue their goal using only a single dominant analogy or model. But this practice seems unduly rigid in biblical interpretation, particularly because the Bible itself sometimes authorizes multiple analogies. We have already seen that the doctrine of the church and the presentation of Christ's messiahship in the Gospels involve more than one dominant motif. We could not rigidly exclude the use of such analogies without implying a criticism of the Bible itself. That course is not acceptable to anyone who believes that the Bible is really the Word of God.

Second, we might argue that biblical interpretation and theology are not analogous to science. This position is, I think, closer to the point. But what kind of biblical interpretation are we talking about? Biblical interpretation of a very practical, down-to-earth kind is continually practiced in the church, by people with and without formal training. Though such interpretation is hardly scientific, as a human activity it does still have some distant relation to science. Some generalities apply pretty well to all activities of human groups and all activities that share human knowledge.[8] But the distant analogy between science and human activity in general does not permit us to impose scientific practice on all of life. Interpretation in a broad sense will continue to make use of the full range of analogies in the Bible and other analogies from modern life as well.

Are different conclusions warranted when we consider the study of the Bible in an intellectually rigorous way? Rigor in biblical interpretation will have greater similarities to the intellectual rigor demanded in scientific activity. But the subject matter of biblical interpretation is different from that of natural science. We are dealing with the Bible and with its teaching, hence with God, humanity, salvation, sin, and many other complex topics. By contrast, the physical aspects of the world are the natural focal topics within natural science. Even the physical aspects of the world are complex and marvelous enough. But a different order of complexity may emerge in the direct study of phenomena involving persons. If human phenomena are innately more complex, it may not be possible to capture them adequately using only one model or analogy.

Of course, some people do try to understand all of human nature from a single starting point, whether that be the economic aspect (Marx), the biological or sexual (Freud), the political, or the aesthetic. Such people sometimes achieve useful insights. But over all, they always misrepresent humanity by reducing and flattening humanity to one dimension.[9]

From a theological point of view, we should not be surprised that human phenomena are difficult to capture through only one dimension. Human beings are made in the image of God. To understand them one must simultaneously understand something of God.[10] And how does one understand

---

[8]See, for example, Peter L. Berger and Thomas Luckmann, *Social Construction of Reality*.(New York: Doubleday, 1966).

[9]On the theme of reductionism, see Dooyeweerd, *New Critique;* and Poythress, *Philosophy, Science, and Sovereignty.*

[10]John Calvin, *Institutes of the Christian Religion* 1.1.1.

God? Through His revelation of Himself. But of course the Bible uses many analogies in speaking of God. He is the great King, the Father of His people, the Maker of heaven and earth, the Judge, the Holy One of Israel (an analogy by way of the holiness code and the holiness of the tabernacle and the priests). He speaks, plans, thinks, loves, hates, blesses, and so on. All these actions are analogous to the actions of human beings. Human beings as the image of God present, in a striking way, many analogies to what God does. But even the other created things speak in a general way of God's everlasting power and deity (Rom. 1:20–21). No one thing in creation is a uniquely suitable standpoint from which and through which to understand God. These verses imply that everything could in some sense be a starting point.

Thus it would appear that, because of the very nature of God and the nature of His relations to creation, there is no one analogy that could claim uniquely to be an adequate starting point for forming a model of God or a theory of God. God is revealed in everything, and yet as the Creator He is unique, unlike anything in creation. We are forbidden to think that we could capture Him with a model. All that the Bible reveals about God and all the ways that it has of speaking, using many analogies, are relevant and profitable. We are to use them all.

It follows, then, that the Bible itself, and the nature of God Himself, keeps us from reducing things to a single model or analogy. This restriction holds true, certainly, in our study of God. But, by analogy, it will be true in a subordinate sense in our study of humanity. Since human beings are made in the image of God, some similar problems present themselves in a study of human beings, particularly as we focus on the all-important question of their relation to God.

In sum, then, there are good reasons for thinking that the subject matter of biblical interpretation presents us with new demands. These demands are not necessarily the same as the demands in natural science. Science may satisfy itself with a single dominant model, but biblical interpretation cannot.

Moreover, one can understand this conclusion also on the practical level. Kuhn identifies some of the social reasons motivating scientists to gravitate toward a single dominant model. If the model appears to be promising and begins to be fruitful in suggesting avenues of research and extensions of its own theory, it is more efficient to follow the one model than to multiply models. Many of the alternatives will prove to be dead ends. The model tends to suggest detailed tests and extensions. In following these, people notice facts that would otherwise escape the most careful observer working without a fixed model. Moreover, when the community of scientists can agree on the overall shape of their field and the ways of making advance, they can go on to treat in great detail the problems that are left. Experience shows that most profit comes from dealing with the remaining problems and by carrying on more and more detailed and extended lines of questioning. By this route, any real long-range inadequacies of the theory will eventually be uncovered. They will not be uncovered by simply casting about wildly in the indefinitely large space of alternate models.

In biblical interpretation, to some extent, analogous observations could be made. The person who has a particular narrow point of view (say, economic or sociological) will often notice things that escape others. The person who analyzes the Bible, attending only to what it says on a single issue (e.g., about God's knowledge), will discover much that might be overlooked by other readers. Therein lies the attractiveness of using a single dominant analogy. The recent stream of theologies illustrates this approach: we have seen theology of the Word, theology of love, theology of hope, theology of liberation, each seizing on a single theme through which to see the whole of theology. But in the long run this approach must be complemented by others, lest the theologian overlook the other analogies that the Bible itself endorses. No one analogy will ever be so uniquely effective in every respect that it has exclusive claim to our attention. By contrast, a scientific model, during periods of normal science, is able to make this claim. The difference in subject matter between science and biblical interpretation therefore explains why the use of a single model is appropriate in one area but not in the other.

The third alternative mentioned above holds that multiple

analogies ought to be used within natural science itself. On a certain level, this practice already occurs. In teaching and in illustration, a scientist may invoke a multiplicity of analogies in explaining theories to an outsider. The quantum theory of light may be introduced by comparing light both to a wave (water wave, sound wave in air, vibration of a string) and to a stream of particles (marbles, water droplets, molecules). But the theory itself, in its inner structure, still has an internal coherence on the basis of extended analogy between certain mathematical equations and the physical world. This state of affairs would thus not seem to get us beyond the use of a single dominant model within the inner core of the theory. (Note, however, that the wave and particle views of light and of elementary particles seemed in the early days of quantum mechanics to be irreconcilable.)

We can still say that the essence of the unity of scientific disciplines is to be found not in the use of a single dominant model but in the unity of a disciplinary matrix. This disciplinary matrix includes models, of course. But it includes standards for judging research success, ideas about what sorts of research are promising, a general framework of assumptions about what the universe is like, concrete exemplars in the form of past definitive results, and so on. Both biblical interpretation as a whole and various subdisciplines could have a coherent disciplinary matrix without sticking to only one analogy in each case.

In fact, we have been arguing here that in many circumstances it is profitable to use first one, then another, analogy in order to learn all that one can about a particular passage or a particular topic in the Bible. The use of multiple analogies could itself become a rule of thumb that would be one element in the disciplinary matrix. In that case, it would serve to unite interpretive method in much the same way that science is united by some rules of thumb about research directions.

Our original question was whether biblical interpretation could justify the use of multiple analogies in contrast to the practice of science. The answer, I believe, is yes. The reasons arise from the differences in subject matter between biblical interpretation and natural science. Of course, the value of using several analogies still does not guarantee that all analogies whatsoever will be fruitful. And we must remember that, if an analogy means introducing false assumptions about God and His world, it can lead us astray. The historical-critical method is the prime example. For similar reasons the recent theologies of hope and of liberation appear to have destructive elements. The Bible has been made to fit into an alien world view by seizing on a theme and reinterpreting it against the background of that world view.

9

LESSONS TO BE LEARNED FROM THE CONTEXTUAL CHARACTER OF KNOWLEDGE

It is time now to take stock of what we have learned. Our concern so far has been primarily to look at natural science and biblical interpretation to understand what is involved in research and theory formation, using Kuhn's work as a stimulus. The main conclusion is that the context of one's assumptions and past knowledge has a profound effect on what one learns in any area of scientific study. Such a context or background includes assumptions about the world, past successes within the discipline (exemplars), tacit guidelines for fruitful areas of future research, and assumptions about the kinds of data that are relevant and valuable.

But should things be going the way they are? Can we improve on the way that biblical interpretation is done? In preceding chapters, I have hinted at some of the answers that I would give. Here we must draw together these evaluations and examine directly the question of how biblical interpretation ought to learn from Kuhn and others who are doing work in the history and philosophy of science.

LEARNING ABOUT BASIC COMMITMENTS OR PRESUPPOSITIONS

First, it is valuable for an exegete or a theologian to be aware of the role of basic commitments or presuppositions in the formation of knowledge. Kuhn and others alert us to the fact that such basic commitments or presuppositions do exist.[1] Exegesis and theological reflection always take place against the background of fundamental assumptions about the nature of the world. They are always motivated by the personal values of the biblical interpreter. Both methods and results are evaluated in terms of standards and epistemological values already presupposed by the interpreter.

At this level, there can be no neutrality. No one evaluates methods or results without standards of evaluation, whether these be explicit or implicit. And not everyone cherishes the same values or the same standards! Often, indeed, there is some overlap in different people's standards. But there are very often subtle differences as well. For example, compare (1) historical standards used by advocates of the historical-critical method and (2) historical standards used by scholarly Evangelicals who view history as the domain of God's providential and occasionally miraculous action. People in both groups are alert to the importance of weighing human testimony and not being credulous. To a degree, both would agree about the psychological and social likelihood of certain kinds of human behavior in certain circumstances. But they differ about what kind of evidence makes miracles credible, because their views of the limits of the world and the prerogatives of historical method differ. Behind this difference, their beliefs differ concerning

---

[1] Presuppositional apologetics, as represented by the work of Cornelius Van Til, has long insisted on the importance of basic commitments (see, e.g., Van Til, *The Defense of the Faith,* 2d ed. [Philadelphia: Presbyterian & Reformed, 1963]). Van Til argues that whether a person is regenerate or unregenerate profoundly influences every aspect of thought and behavior. Believers presuppose that God exists, rules the world, and governs all facts; that human beings are abnormal since the Fall; that human beings must find their standards for criticism, evaluation, and truth in God. Unbelievers presuppose the opposite. But believers are inconsistent because of their remaining sinfulness, while unbelievers are inconsistent because they must carry on in God's world, in which order and standards so clearly exist but do not derive from finite humanity or finite idols. These basic presuppositions affect people's interaction with every fact of experience, every human attitude, and every proposed criterion for evaluation.

what allegiance to God requires of someone engaged in intellectual reflection.

Some people use the idea of basic commitments as an excuse for complacency. They think that, since everyone is committed to something, they have as much right to their commitments as anyone else. But precisely because basic commitments are basic, it is important that people have the right ones. These commitments will affect everything that they do. And though, by common grace, they may do some helpful things in spite of bad basic commitments, their actions will be tainted by these same commitments.

Even we who have Christian commitments must not be complacent. We know that our motives are contaminated by sin. Sometimes we are aware of sinful motivations and assumptions, but other times, even when we are missing the mark, we may easily deceive ourselves into thinking that our basic commitments are fully biblical and in accord with God's standards.

We must remember that, though the Bible is infallible, our own understanding of the Bible is not. Hence some practice of critical self-doubt, in the light of the Bible's searchlight, is in order. As long as this doubting criticizes ourselves, rather than doubting God or doubting the Bible as God's Word, we are acting in conformity with Christian standards.

Moreover, we cannot be complacent about persuading others to adopt our basic commitments. Unfortunately, sometimes people do become complacent. They argue that, since each person evaluates evidence in the light of their basic commitments, it is useless to argue with anyone. Others will just use their own standards. They will not accept any argument given on the basis of Christian standards.

Basic commitments are indeed at stake here. Arguments with non-Christians are frequently not easy. We are sometimes tempted to give up or to compromise by adopting standards based on alien basic commitments. How, then, do we remain persuasive while not compromising? Although whole books are needed to deal with these issues, we can note here a few simple elements in the solution.[2] Everyone lives in God's world, and no one can escape that world or the knowledge of God that impresses itself on creatures in God's image (Rom. 1:18–22). Argument is not futile, because the facts are on our side, the standards that are truly legitimate are on our side, and—most importantly—the Holy Spirit works to break down people's resistance to the truth.

Moreover, people can also be challenged concerning the idolatrous character of their basic commitments. Whenever people have basic commitments to anything other than God and His Word, they are practicing a subtle form of idolatry. They are often attempting to escape responsibility for submitting to God. Christ died in order to free us from these sins as well as others. We may command people to repent of these sins, just as the apostles commanded people to repent.

But awareness of basic commitments has relevance for more than just carrying on argument. The fundamental value of this awareness is that it enables us to evaluate our own work and the work of others on more than one level. We can evaluate people's work both in terms of the basic commitments that motivate it and in terms of the value of its individual parts and details. Sometimes both the basic commitments and the details are good. Sometimes both are bad. But sometimes sloppy work comes from people with good commitments, or high-quality work from people with bad commitments. Sometimes there is a complex mixture of good and bad in several areas.

Awareness of the influence of basic commitments makes us better able to discern the effects that good or bad commitments have had on scholarly work, and so to make adjustments. We will not be swept off our feet by a highly insightful work showing effects of bad commitments. We will be able to learn from the insights, while noticing places where the bad commitments have infected the product. Conversely, we will not be impressed by mediocre work from those with good commit-

---

[2]For a clear introduction to the problem, see Frame, "God and Biblical Language," pp. 159–77. For an extended exposition, see John M. Frame, *The Doctrine of the Knowledge of God,* (Phillipsburg, NJ: Presbyterian and Reformed, 1987).

ments. We will be able to honor the good commitments that a person has, while not ignoring the faults of the resulting ideas.

Finally, awareness of the importance of basic commitments and their resistance to refutation should make us all the more aware of our finiteness and of our need for divine verbal revelation from the Bible. We never rise above our basic commitments. They control us and our interpretation more than we control them. In particular, human beings determined to escape from God's authority and to be their own gods can generate basic commitments, but they do so merely by projecting their own finite guesses into the infinite. They make idols that subsequently enslave them. To reform and purify our basic commitments from our sin and idolatry, we need a clear word from God expressing the content of the standards, a divine power of the Spirit transforming us, and a divine Savior from God cleansing us. In other words, we need just the richness of salvation that the message of Scripture promises and bestows.

LEARNING THAT FACTS ARE THEORY-LADEN

Another area from which we can learn is Kuhn's discussion of the role of facts in natural science. All facts, according to Kuhn, are theory-laden. That is, the facts are not strictly objective, the same for everyone, regardless of their disciplinary framework. Rather, the facts are subtly different depending on who is looking at them. The relative importance of a fact, its relevance and even whether it counts as a fact at all, depends on the view of the world and the standards contained in a disciplinary framework.

To be sure, not everyone within the history and philosophy of science agrees with Kuhn. Opponents of Kuhn are uneasy with the provocative language that he uses. They would disagree with some of his formulations and prefer to stress the ways in which the history of science shows considerable common ground between differing disciplinary matrices with respect to some kinds of facts.[3]

But Kuhn does not mean that competing disciplinary frameworks have no way of talking to one another. Usually there will be many facts on which they agree. But the difference in framework may result in subtle differences in how those facts are seen. There is no perfect separation between fact and interpretation; facts always exist against a background view of the world. People in different frameworks therefore frequently use key words in different ways. Communication between two different disciplinary frameworks may resemble a work of translation.

Moreover, one cannot single out beforehand a special domain of pure facts that must be accepted and accounted for by any scientific theory whatsoever. In science, the typical facts are the results of instrumental measurements and presuppose at least a theory of the instruments. In addition, anomalies (i.e., phenomena that do not fit into the framework of existing theory) are frequently ignored until for some reason—controlled by the disciplinary framework—they draw the attention of scientists.

Even if Kuhn is not entirely right about science, there is something here for biblical interpreters to learn. Biblical interpretation deals first of all with the concrete tests of Scripture. In addition, all interpretation in one way or another interacts with the modern world. In some cases the facts of the modern world can be left in the background. Interpretation that is interacting with questions of application will, however, be directly concerned with the facts about the modern world.

Such facts are typically about churches, human beliefs, philosophy, and economic, social, and political structures. But how does one gather facts? Does one rely on individual personal spiritual experience, personal contacts, statistical surveys, social critics, or Marxist class analysis? Clearly, gathering facts is

---

[3] See, for example, Dudley Shapere, "Meaning and Scientific Change," in *Scientific Revolutions,* ed. Ian Hacking (Oxford: Oxford University Press, 1981), pp. 28–59.

influenced by one's world view and what sorts of facts one counts as important. The supposed fact of a person's membership in a particular socioeconomic class is a fact only if one first accepts such classes as an objective reality rather than merely a theoretical construct.

Even when we come to the study of the biblical text, we are not free from these difficulties. Careful study of the Bible requires some attention to the historical and cultural environments in which particular books of the Bible were written (at least if our framework of assumptions tells us that the original historical setting is relevant to interpretation!). Getting facts about these environments is again conditioned by one's methods and disciplinary framework. Practitioners of the historical-critical method have sometimes inferred whole social movements, schools, and literary sources on the basis of scant evidence. When the evidence is scant, the role of overall assumptions is even greater than usual.

When we come to the text of Scripture itself, it might be thought that everyone agrees on the facts. Everyone agrees that certain Hebrew and Greek letters occur in a certain order in the received text (ignoring textual criticism). But it is easy to show that, beyond a very elementary level, the same phenomena are interpreted very differently within different disciplinary frameworks. For example, traditional historical-critical method uses the facts of aporias (apparent tensions or contradictions) and sudden transitions ("seams") in the biblical text as evidence for different sources. Traditional inerrantist method uses these same facts as a starting point for an investigation of harmonization. Newer literary approaches use the same facts as key clues to the techniques of literary artistry and subtlety.

Moreover, the text itself is not an object of study in the same way within different disciplinary frameworks. Traditional historical-critical method treats the text as merely one layer in a tradition. According to this method, the text has earlier sources and traditions as well as later evolutions. No particular special status is to be assigned to the text itself, except that by historical accident it, rather than its sources or its later evolutions, has survived.

On the other hand, traditional inerrantist method treats the text as part of a whole canon, all of which is the Word of God and in principle harmonizable. Some texts may have sources (e.g., Luke may have used Mark), but even then the sources are irrelevant to the meaning and authority of the final product.

Newer literary approaches sometimes abstract the text from its environment. They may ignore the sources and later uses valued by the historical-critical method. They may choose equally to ignore the references to historical events valued by Evangelicals. They treat the material simply as a product of literary artistry, ignoring its straightforward truth claims in favor of finding a kind of artistic or aesthetic truth in its manner of expression.[4]

In sum, the facts receive vastly different treatment, depending on which disciplinary frameworks they fall under. And we have looked only at disciplinary frameworks that are in current widespread use. We have not talked about the medieval framework for exegesis or theology, or a framework that might be generated by Buddhism or Islam.

In one respect, the influence of basic commitments is being recapitulated here. Basic commitments are bound to influence the development of any disciplinary framework, including methods of approach to the biblical text and to modern facts. Historically speaking, basic commitments certainly did influence the development of the historical-critical method, traditional inerrantist method, newer literary methods, theology of liberation, and so on. But the influence sometimes goes the other way as well. A disciplinary framework can influence the basic commitments of those involved with it.

A disciplinary framework has a momentum of its own, a record of success, that sometimes appeals to people with different basic commitments. People adopt the framework because of its successes, without studying whether the frame-

---

[4]See Tremper Longman, III, *Literary Approaches to Biblical Interpretation,* Foundations of Contemporary Interpretation, vol. 3 (Grand Rapids: Zondervan, 1987).

work itself assumes or encourages a certain set of basic commitments. Then, as they immerse themselves in the framework, they find that their basic commitments themselves undergo subtle (or violent) change under the influence of hidden assumptions that they begin to adopt consciously or unconsciously.

Moreover, what counts as a fact has a subtle influence. If one is immersed in an environment where a single disciplinary framework is being used, one is constantly confronted with the facts that the framework considers especially revealing. One is made to feel that such facts do reveal something. To deny what they reveal is to "ignore the facts." Hence people are swept along into conformity with the framework, usually without ever adequately examining how a competing framework might treat the same "facts."

This kind of influence of disciplinary frameworks is not merely hypothetical. Students at a seminary operating exclusively under the framework of the historical-critical method are often exposed only to the critical historical reconstructions of Israelite history, the supposed contradictions in the Bible showing its historically limited character, and theologies of revelation that have adjusted themselves to these viewpoints. Conversely, students at a conservative Evangelical seminary may be exposed only to historical explanations and theology of revelation compatible with verbal inspiration. Some seminaries, of course, make an effort at wider exposure, but the professors will naturally spend by far the most time on those points of view that they themselves think have some positive contribution or some hope of being right.

What lesson can we learn here? One must not, indeed, "ignore the facts." But every research framework is confronted with anomalies that are difficult to explain. Every research framework tends to talk about its successes and to concentrate on problems that the method has some hope of solving, rather than on what is most intractable. If one is trying to choose between disciplinary frameworks or is trying to modify an existing framework, one must avoid being intimidated by people who appeal to "the facts." Such people are most often thinking of those facts that (they think) prove their case. Other facts, less easily explained, are not mentioned.

EVALUATING COMPETING RESEARCH PROGRAMS IN BIBLICAL INTERPRETATION

We can also learn some lessons about the possibility of evaluating competing schools in biblical interpretation and research. Does Kuhn's idea of scientific progress through revolutions help us? How do we judge whether one of two competing schools is the more fruitful?

From Kuhn we learn that evaluation is not easy. Kuhn points out that, when a new exemplar appears, it appears as a theory in the process of development, not as a finished product. It may explain only experimental results in a tiny field but be unable to explain the great body of facts covered by a theory already in existence. Only time can tell whether a fresh idea can be developed far enough and fruitfully enough to supersede a theory already dominating the field.

Hence Kuhn does not think that his analysis provides any basis for prejudging the success of new ideas or theories. For evaluating new ideas, the practitioners in the field are the best judges.[5] Often people are presented with a choice between two disciplinary frameworks, both of which have some strengths and some weaknesses. The difficulty in making a choice is not surprising. If only one framework had strengths, only it would have a significant number of adherents, and we would not be thinking about how to choose between two frameworks.

Suppose two disciplinary frameworks vie for our attention and allegiance. One disciplinary framework has a long record of success. But it is now struggling with growing areas of anomalies that so far have been integrated into the framework only with difficulty or not at all. Nevertheless, because of its record of past success, it is rational to hope that continued effort might succeed in explaining the anomalies.

The second framework, by contrast, is new. It is a

---

[5] Kuhn, *Structure of Scientific Revolutions,* p. 200.

modification of the old one, and so hopes to build on the successes of the old framework. But it has not yet succeeded in explaining the whole field that the old framework covered so well. It has no long track record. However, it shows promise because it has done better in accounting for some of the anomalies that have come to trouble the old framework. It is rational, then, to hope that continued effort might enable people to succeed in using the new approach to explain everything explained by the old framework, and the anomalies as well.

While tension between frameworks takes place within science, one can see something resembling this dynamic process in biblical interpretation as well. When the historical-critical method first began to arise, it was an inchoate framework in comparison with the established dogmatic, supernaturalistic frameworks. The initial developers of the historical-critical method did not explain all the details of the Bible with nearly the thoroughness attained by later practitioners. They were followed because of hopes that the evolutionary and naturalistic assumptions that gave a certain coherent picture of the modern world and of certain aspects of biblical religion would in the end provide a more satisfactory picture of everything.

The historical-critical method is one case of successful development of a new disciplinary framework—successful in the sense that it gradually came to be a dominating framework in scholarly circles. Arianism, in contrast, is an example of a failure. It was eventually rejected by the mainstream of the church, although at one time it gained many adherents and continues to have periodic revivals in liberalism and cults.

We may also note that scientific theories thought to be outmoded may experience revival later on. The corpuscular theory of light gained dominance from Newton's time onward. It was superseded by the wave theory in the nineteenth century, and then corpuscular aspects of light were reintroduced in the twentieth century in connection with the development of quantum theory. From this instance one can see that the historical eclipse of a point of view does not guarantee its long-range invalidity.

One suspects that similar changes may occur even more

often in biblical interpretation and in the humanities than in science. In biblical interpretation and humanities basic commitments about the nature of human beings have had more direct influence on the nature of theory building and disciplinary frameworks. Alterations in basic commitments over the centuries may result in the dominance of first one, then another, interpretive school, without proving the superiority of the later results over the earlier. Moreover, because of the multifaceted character of human beings, as people made in God's image, more than one type of explanation can account for a large number of facts. For example, there can be economic, sociological, psychological, political, and religious explanations. Such explanations have actually been offered for the events of the Reformation, and all of the explanations have some plausibility.

Even the domination of a single disciplinary framework for a long time may show mainly the dominant attraction of an ideology, a philosophy, or a world view more than the inherent superiority of the framework. Marxism dominates scholarly analysis of religion in the communist world partly because of its appeal as a world view and its importance in supporting the present political structures. Likewise, one may suggest, the historical-critical method has dominated Christian scholarship for so long, partly because it supports the ideology of naturalism, which has dominated Western thought since the Enlightenment.

One cannot, of course, prove scientifically that an inerrantist approach to Scripture is superior to the mainstream historical-critical approach. Showing in detail how an inerrantist approach makes sense of the data is important. But the differences between these two frameworks touch on one's deepest religious commitments. In evaluation, one must appeal to those commitments. And one must appeal to the hope for future success as well, since the present successes of a framework may not fully reveal its future potential. Evangelicals know that the future ultimately leads to the second coming of Christ. The Second Coming will be the ultimate place for revealing success or failure of disciplinary frameworks investigating Scripture. Because we base our hopes on God's promises, it is rational to think that at that point an Evangelical framework will be seen to be superior.

I have used examples from biblical interpretation that represent rather deep-seated cleavages. But something can also be said about differences that are less serious. Consider only Evangelical interpretation. Among Evangelicals there is a good measure of agreement on the basic teachings of the Bible and on hermeneutical principles. Hence there are also standards to which we may appeal in evaluating theological innovations and competitions between different schools. Even with such a measure of agreement, however, we confront some complexities.

For example, suppose that we are evaluating a new interpretation of Romans 7. A new idea, one that is just getting off the ground, may have greater promise, both because it has not been worked on yet and because it has apparently shed light on some difficulty in the Bible. In this case, the new interpretation claims to shed light on the difficulty of dealing with the language of Romans 7. But it is likely to be only weakly integrated with dominant theological systems. If it cannot succeed in integrating the insights of older theology, it may just spawn error or even heresy. In the particular case of Romans 7, Lloyd-Jones's interpretation might lead to the idea that there was, ontologically, a third category of people distinct from regenerate or unregenerate. (This is not what Lloyd-Jones means, but one can see how someone else might further develop his approach.)

A new idea always has to compete with the older approaches. The strength of the older approaches is that they have thoroughly worked through the details of biblical passages and that they are more thoroughly integrated with whole theological systems. People might prefer an older explanation because of this very thoroughness.

In such situations there is no easy answer. Whenever new ideas or new approaches arise, we must evaluate them. Evaluation takes into account their potential for future development, not just their present adequacy (or deficiency). But we must also take into account the fact that an older approach offers actual explanations at some points where a new approach may remain only a potential hope. Even when people have similar standards (as the community of Evangelicals does), they may reasonably disagree about the relative merits of two approaches to a difficulty. This disagreement in turn will lead to differences in judgment about whether it is more worthwhile to spend time in developing a new approach or to reinforce and enhance an old one.

10

USING PERSPECTIVES

Let us now examine whether differences in disciplinary frameworks must always lead to a competition between different schools and the eventual triumph of one school. Can we sometimes incorporate insights from different points of view into a richer whole?

DEALING WITH DIFFERING POINTS OF VIEW

Recall first, that, according to Kuhn, sciences begin their history in a preparadigm, or immature, stage. In this situation a number of schools compete for dominance, and no particular way of formulating the problems or of moving toward solutions is so superior to its rivals that it effectively drives them from the field. According to Kuhn, this stage cannot be eliminated. One cannot simply choose one school and ignore the others, because one does not know which school will produce the most effective advance in science in the long run. The immature stage comes to an end only when a superior theory or exemplar arises within one school or when features from several schools are combined. One cannot hasten this process. One cannot simply decree that a superior theory will arise now rather than later.

One might liken biblical interpretation to an immature

science. In systematic theology, even if some theological system is dominant for a time, it does not permanently banish its rivals. The history of millennial theories illustrates this fact. One can see the same thing even in the history of christological controversies. In a sense the Nicene Creed and the Chalcedonian creed set forth exemplars that obtain dominance and form the basis for subsequent reflection. One might thus argue that these creeds represent turning points toward mature christology and mature Trinitarianism.

But forms of Arianism have cropped up again and again through the ages, up until modern times. They are never permanently eradicated by orthodoxy. In this case, I would say that non-Arian orthodoxy is correct, but Arianism is never permanently eliminated because it appeals to sinful tendencies in human nature that would subject God to tight, over-simplified rationalistic categories. The Trinity and the Incarnation are permanent offenses to such autonomous human reasoning.

The example of Arianism shows that sometimes we cannot hope to combine rival schools. To try to synthesize Trinitarian theology with Arianism is to try to combine truth and error. Of course, a revival of Arianism might conceivably arise in reaction to one-sided orthodoxy. If orthodox theologians in emphasizing the deity of Christ lose sight of His humanity, they will eventually provoke a reaction by people who rediscover Christ's humanity. This rediscovery may overreact by eliminating Christ's deity. If we lived through such a situation, it would behoove us to note the problems on both sides. Sometimes the side that is in the wrong may yet be grasping at a fragment of truth ignored by the side that is basically in the right.

In the area of hermeneutics, similarly, we might argue that one interpretive system has never obtained absolute dominance and completely superseded all others. The historical-critical method has dominated biblical exegesis for at least a century, but it never completely eliminated inerrantist approaches and traditional Roman Catholic approaches. The Reformers championed grammatical-historical interpretation over against medieval allegorical interpretation, but allegorical interpretation never completely disappeared from the churches that derived from the Reformation.[1]

MULTIPLE APPROACHES TO TRUTH

Must we say that all differences in biblical interpretation and in theology are differences between truth and error? Are they all like the difference between Arianism and Trinitarianism? No. Sometimes the differences are like the difference between viewing the church as the temple of God and viewing it as the body of Christ. Clearly we have to do here with complementary truths rather than opposition between truth and error. The difference here is a difference between two perspectives on the same truths.

In such a situation, each perspective is better at seeing and emphasizing certain truths of Scripture. Hence it would seem advisable to use a multiplicity of perspectives. As we have seen, this use of multiple perspectives can be valuable even when we are dealing with a passage such as 1 Corinthians 3:10–15, where one analogy dominates in the text. After determining what analogy, if any, is indeed dominant in a given passage of Scripture, we should not hesitate to see how other biblical analogies illumine the same passage. Such a procedure may alert us to neglected features of the passage. (For example, the role of fire in 1 Cor. 3:10–15 is illuminated when we use the biblical picture of God as Judge rather than confining ourselves simply to the analogy between church and temple.) Use of some other analogy will almost certainly make us more aware of connections between the passage that we are studying and the many other passages of the Bible that use the analogy that we have chosen.

We can extend these observations still further. As I have argued at length in another place,[2] there is value not only in using a variety of analogies but in trying to extend the

---

[1] See Moisés Silva, *Has the Church Misread the Bible? The History of Interpretation in the Light of Current Issues,* Foundations of Contemporary Interpretation, vol. 1 (Grand Rapids: Zondervan, 1987).

[2] Poythress, *Symphonic Theology.*

analogies, to enrich them, until they are huge theories or explanations that can cover all facts of Scripture. We start with a single biblical analogy or motif like the temple or the judge. Then we view all of the Bible through the spectacles of this one motif. In the process, we try to enrich the motif itself so as to include and explain things that were originally not thought to be related to it. It is as if we pretended that we were going to form our own theological school and that this school would put forth a scientific theory of theology based on a single coherent model that was in turn some form of our starting analogy or a modification or enrichment of it.

This procedure is really not so dissimilar to the way a scientific theory originates. Scientists work with suggestive analogies or models that they tinker with and modify as they go. For example, Maxwell invokes a model in reflecting on his researches leading to the famous equations of electromagnetic theory:

> By referring everything to the purely geometrical idea of the motion of an imaginary fluid, I hope to attain generality and precision, and to avoid the dangers arising from a premature theory professing to explain the cause of the phenomena. . . . The substance here treated of . . . is not even a hypothetical fluid which is introduced to explain actual phenomena. It is merely a collection of imaginary properties which may be employed for establishing certain theorems in pure mathematics in a way more intelligible to many minds and more applicable to physical problems than that in which algebraic symbols alone are used.[3]

Maxwell thus begins using the model of a fluid in order to suggest a series of connections between mathematical equations and the physical object (electromagnetism). The analogy suggests certain lines of development mathematically. Such development would not have been easy if one were dealing only with the results of previous investigation without simplifying or organizing them.[4]

---

[3] James Clerk Maxwell, *The Scientific Papers of James Clerk Maxwell* (Cambridge: Cambridge University Press, 1890), pp. 159–60.

[4] Ibid., pp. 155–56.

In the case of biblical research, one may argue that there are even stronger reasons for utilizing analogies. For one thing, the analogies that I consider here are presented in one form or another within the Bible itself. We know that these are good analogies, albeit of a limited character. Physical scientists, by contrast, must cast about on their own for analogies from the physical world. They have not been told directly by God which analogies will work.

One relatively successful example of just this procedure is the history of covenant theology. Covenant theology in its mature form is capable of viewing all of God's relations with human beings, and even the redemptive counsel between the Father and the Son, in terms of analogies with the concrete covenants of the Bible. At the start of the process, theologians observe that the Hebrew and Greek equivalents of the word *covenant* are used in the Bible to draw an analogy between relations of God and human beings and treaties between human beings. This analogy is then stretched and generalized, and the word *covenant* becomes a technical term filled with all the ideas developed by comparing a large number of passages that speak about God's relation to human beings.[5]

Covenant theology in fact succeeds in integrating, explaining, and organizing into a coherent whole the vast sweep of biblical revelation. But it does so partly by enriching the idea of covenant. The word *covenant* within theological vocabulary is now related by a rich series of connotations to the entire complex of biblical revelation about the relation of God to human beings through history.

People who are used to thinking in terms of covenant theology may not think that there are really alternatives. In a sense, if covenant theology is right, there are no other

[5] See Meredith G. Kline, *The Structure of Biblical Authority* (Grand Rapids: Eerdmans, 1972); idem, *Treaty of the Great King: The Covenant Structure of Deuteronomy*. (Grand Rapids: Eerdmans, 1963); idem, *Kingdom Prologue*, 2 vols. (South Hamilton, Mass.: Meredith G. Kline, 1981–83); John Murray, "Covenant Theology," in *The Encyclopedia of Christianity,* ed. Philip E. Hughes (Marshallton, Del.: National Foundation for Christian Education, 1972), 3:199–219.

alternatives. That is, no system contradicting covenant theology can possibly be right. But a contradictory system is not the only alternative—there could also be complementary ways of expounding the *same* truths. If we chose to do it another way, there would be differences of emphasis or differences in organization, but no contradiction.

For example, we could develop the whole theological system in terms of the theme of God's family, and the relation of God as Father to His people as children. Surely the theme of fatherhood and family is an important theme in Scripture, and surely it touches on the heart of God's purposes and His intentions as much as does covenant theology.

One might reply that covenant theology has already achieved this result. To talk about God's fatherly relation to His people is simply to talk about His covenant with His people, no more and no less. Both sides are talking about the same thing, no doubt. But there are still different ways of talking, and the different ways bring to the fore different aspects of biblical teaching. The idea of covenant within covenant theology has definite legal associations, while the idea of family suggests first of all social, emotional, and personal relations. If we use only one of these types of vocabulary, we will have to be careful somewhere along the line to alert people to complementary truths. For example, if we used *covenant* to include everything, we would have to say that the word is intended (unlike its use outside of God-human relationships) to connote all the familial ideas. Or vice versa, if we used the idea of family as our central organizational idea, we would have to say that the idea of family is intended to include a legal side of adoption, whereby according to God's standards we who were castaways have been given the legal rights of family members.

Because covenant theology has a long history of development, it may seem more natural to view the family ideas in the Bible as a metaphorical or analogical expression of one aspect of covenant. According to this viewpoint, God's covenant is the basic underlying reality. Expressions using family ideas bring out one aspect of the covenant. But let us ask ourselves what might have happened if the history of theology had been different. What if the idea of familial theology had been developed with great thoroughness? What if someone now made the bizarre suggestion that we should redo the whole of the theological enterprise using covenant (a comparatively lesser-used theme in theology) as the center point?

I anticipate that we would find some die-hard advocates of familial theology who would resist the idea that covenant could ever have the centrality that the idea of God's family clearly had. They would say something like this:

> The familial relation between God as Father and the people of God as His children is the underlying reality. This relation is nothing less than a reflection on the creaturely level of the Trinitarian relation between the Father and the Son. What could be deeper than that? Covenants in the Bible are used as analogical or metaphorical expressions for one aspect of this family relation, namely the aspect of legal privilege, fatherly requirements, and obedience expected of children. Familial theology already includes these aspects. We do not ignore the covenants. Clearly familial theology has already done the job that this newfangled covenant theology proposes to do. Familial theology has already uncovered the real nature of the relation of God to human beings. The proposed covenant theology shifts things away from this center. Hence it will have a subtly incorrect emphasis. At the same time, it will achieve nothing new, since familial theology already includes an account of covenants.

Do we need to choose between covenant theology and familial theology? Is one of these superior in every respect? Or are they equivalent? It would seem that they are closer to being equivalent. Each has a natural tendency to a different emphasis (legal vs. social/personal), but there is no disharmony. A good theologian working with either of these starting points will eventually notice in Scripture all the aspects of God's relation to human beings.

Unfortunately, we are not all good theologians. Or at least we do not always find it so easy to notice everything that the Bible says. Some people sitting under the teaching of covenant theology have understood God's covenant in a merely legal, one might say legalistic, way. They have missed the personal dimension of relationship to God. They have not really been affected by the fact that God is our Father. This overlooking of the personal dimension is contrary to the intentions and express teaching of the great covenant theologians. But it sometimes happens anyway. Conversely, one might imagine that, if familial theology dominated history, some people would not realize that God had rules—yes, laws. They would misconstrue the familial relation as lawless, in spite of the intentions of the greatest familial theologians.

Hence I conclude that, since we do not always observe everything and see all the angles, it is perhaps better not to put all our eggs in one basket. That is to say, it is better not to use only one analogy or theme as the route by which we approach biblical interpretation. If we do, we may miss something. The situation in theology is vaguely analogous to the situation with the wave and particle theories of light. Within quantum theory the two approaches achieve a reconciliation in principle. But some particular phenomena concerning light show more prominently one aspect rather than the other, and one viewpoint is frequently more useful than another for making a particular analysis. Similarly, in the Bible there is harmony between viewing God's relation to human beings as a covenant and viewing it as a relation between father and son. But some particular passages of the Bible show one aspect more prominently, and one viewpoint may be more useful for making a particular point or noticing particular features of a text.

The use of multiple perspectives must itself be qualified as one approach among many. Within the body of Christ, different people have different gifts. Perhaps, because of our natural disposition or the background that God has given to us, we will use only one theme ourselves. We perhaps understand one approach better, and we are more familiar with it. But we must be ready to listen to other people in the body of Christ whom God has gifted in other ways. Men have to listen to women and women to men; scholars to non-scholars and vice versa; Americans to Latinos and vice versa.

We therefore must listen to other people with other perspectives. Listening to people does not mean that we must tolerate whatever we hear or whatever someone else does; we are not to be complacent about sin or error. But neither are we to be quick to brand something as sin or error, before listening enough to find out whether a complementary perspective may be involved. The earlier example of Arianism shows that we must sometimes draw a clear line. But the example of covenant theology versus familial theology shows equally that we must not have a hair-trigger intolerance. Only growth in discernment, love, and knowledge of God's Word will enable us to succeed more and more effectively in building up the body of Christ in the truth (Eph. 4:15–16; cf. Phil. 1:9–11).

11

BIBLICAL INTERPRETATION REORGANIZED USING DIFFERENT PERSPECTIVES

In practice, how can we reorganize the entire system of biblical interpretation in terms of a new perspective? What happens when we deliberately set about to use a new analogy? It is difficult to work out an example thoroughly within a short space. Such a reorganization might easily involve writing one or more whole books of systematic theology or biblical theology.

THEMATIC REORGANIZATION

Among non-Evangelical theologies one can find examples of work that has nearly attempted reorganizing biblical interpretation in terms of a new theme. We can find numerous theologies that are organized in terms of a single theme chosen as the dominant one: theology of liberation, theology of hope (Moltmann), theology of the future, theology of human existence (Bultmann). The fact that most of these theologies are gross distortions might seem to argue strongly against the wisdom or legitimacy of doing "thematic" theology. The grave danger, however, lies not in the mere fact of organizing theology around a theme. It lies in the fact that, if one understands the theme itself in an unbiblical way, this unbiblical understanding can then easily penetrate the whole texture of the theology rather than being confined to one part.

But one might also see an advantage here. For all their distortions, non-Evangelical thematic theologies sometimes include bits of insight and truth, sometimes uncovering logical and thematic linkages in the Bible that are really there. They are often close enough to the truth to seem plausible and to capture followers.

Naturally, part of the solution to the problem of distorted thematic theologies lies in critical observations to the effect that the central theme of the theology is itself understood in a distorted and unbiblical way. Such critical observations are useful and necessary. But there is room also for reworking the whole theology the right way, by starting with the same theme understood now in a genuinely biblical way.

LIBERATION AS A THEME

Thus, for example, in imitation of liberation theology one can indeed argue that the whole of the biblical record can be understood as a record of God's liberating deeds. But in the Bible the deepest liberation is liberation from sin and the kingdom of Satan. Changes in political and social structures, though significant, are secondary to this most basic liberation. In this light, the present-day theologies of liberation, insofar as they reduce liberation to a purely horizontal and human level, not only truncate the richness of biblical liberation but are in danger of reversing it.[1] However much it may appeal to religious language, the "liberation" set in motion by political education and action will be tainted with autosoterism. The folly that thinks that people (conceived now as social human beings rather than individual beings) must save themselves is itself the beginning of bondage, not true liberation.

By reorganizing theology under the theme of liberation,

---

[1] I recognize that the situation in theology of liberation is complex and that I cannot claim to offer a thoroughgoing critique in this context. Not all the work under the banner of theology of liberation is merely horizontal in character. But to the degree that Marxist social and economic analysis dominates, reductionistic horizontalizing tendencies are inevitable. Marx assumed that society can be scientifically analyzed without reference to God.

we might show, for example, that the Marxist-oriented theologies of liberation are not the only way in which one might plausibly appeal to an important biblical theme. But we might also learn something that our earlier interpretation of the Bible had neglected, namely, that God's liberation of His people does include a corporate social and political dimension, not merely the salvation of individual souls. We would have enriched and reformed not only the theology of liberation but also our own previous practice of interpretation.

MONEY AS A THEME

Second, let us take the theme of money as a dominant theme around which to organize the whole of biblical interpretation. At first glance such a reorganization might seem difficult or impossible. Money is a prominent theme in the Gospels, but most of the remarks about it seem to be negative! How could one make these negative comments the starting point of a positive theology?

I have in mind here using money as a perspective on the *whole* of biblical interpretation, not simply picking out from the whole of theology whatever tidbits have implications in the area of economics. We are looking for a kind of "monetary theology" corresponding to theology of liberation or theology of hope.

When we start with what seems to be an unpromising theme one of the first helpful things to do is to expand or enrich the starting theme. That is, we redefine it or enlarge it so that the enlargement suggests an increasing number of connections with many passages and themes of the Bible. In the case of money, we are dealing with some means of exchange for wealth and for valuable things. Typically this means of exchange has been socially and politically agreed upon. In short, money is not just a piece of paper or a round piece of metal. Its meaning is closely connected with its use in facilitating the exchange of valuable materials. It is a symbolic means for designating and exchanging wealth and valuables.

Hence we can make the step of expanding or enriching the

theme of money by redefining it as the theme of means for exchange of wealth and value. From there it is only a short step to seeing the potential for a God-centered approach to money. In the beginning God has all wealth and all value. When He creates the world, He produces wealth and value from His own fullness and bounty. The world belongs to Him. He owns it. All wealth, all value, is therefore in a fundamental sense God's. God's creation and providence are thus the point of origin for all of our understanding of money.

God has created the world for His own glory. That purpose involves also the multiplication of wealth within the world, including wealth given to His creatures and in particular to human beings made in God's image. The money of human beings is a product of their abilities given by God to subdue the world and fill it with His wealth. Certain created substances, such as silver and gold, are suited from the beginning for such use. The human ability to produce fresh meanings and significance leads to their agreeing to establish a precise economic significance for particular manufactured objects like coins.

These abilities and actions on the part of human beings are reflections on a creaturely level of abilities of God. God is the original Creator of wealth, value, silver, gold, and the symbolic significance of each thing. Human beings are derivatively creative, as imitators of God. The original wealth is the fullness of God's own all-sufficiency and bounty. The original from which human money derives is the symbolic significance that God gives to His wealth: it signifies God Himself.

Moreover, we have observed that human money is a symbolic means for facilitating exchange of value. God Himself is the originator of all means. In fact, the whole creation is a means for producing the exchange of His glory (i.e., wealth!) with human beings. The history of the world is nothing less than the history of "money," in this tremendously expanded sense of the word.

Starting from our newly expanded concept of money, we can more easily see how a whole approach to biblical interpretation and theology could be built up around the theme of money. God Himself is source of both wealth and money in the extended sense. God's law is the money (i.e., the means of facilitating exchange of wealth) for regulating the conduct of human beings. God's redemption is His paying the price of the life of His own Son in exchange (a monetary transaction) for the lives of sinful people. The purpose of human life is to accumulate wealth (namely, the inheritance of God Himself and God's kingdom; see Matt. 6:33). They store up "treasure in heaven" (Luke 12:33–34). At the same time they are to do all for the glory of God, that is, for the increase of His praise (a form of wealth or value). All their service is means (money) toward these goals. Money in the narrow sense is simply one means among many. Within this framework we may then proceed to translate various passages of the Bible into the terminology of our monetary theology.

What use is it to interpret the Bible in this way? For one thing, it may help us to see that the use of money in the narrow sense is not an isolated issue. Nor are the commandments arbitrary that God gives concerning the use of money. The use of money is related to the totality of God's purposes for the world and for human beings in the world.

A second possible use would be in connection with people whose ideas about money are not fully biblical. In the United States in certain quarters, a theology of wealth has taken hold, a popularized theology that tells people that God wants them to be rich. This pseudotheology does not speak of the Atonement or of the necessity of criticism of worldly standards, but only of a Jesus who wants them to be happy and of how they can promote their happiness and wealth by believing in Him.

We might choose to attack this perverse theology in many ways. But one way that most orthodox Evangelicals would not immediately think of would be to "steal the thunder" of theology of wealth by emphasizing their own theme of wealth. Does this capitulate to their perversion? Not if we enrich our idea of wealth in the way that I have sketched out above. Then we may say,

> Indeed Jesus wants us to be wealthy! But what is wealth? Are the most valuable things always those that are manufactured in

American society? Who is the most wealthy person of all? God Himself. What does He say about wealth? His wealth is first of all in His character. He undertakes to spread His wealth abroad by reproducing His character in us. The law of God is a recipe for imitating God and, in so doing, being transformed into a wealthy person. But initially we have too much poverty to keep God's law. It takes money to make money. So God sent His own Son, who became poor for our sake, in order that we might become rich. Riches now mean investing in character conforming to Christ, including sharing in His suffering, so that we may enjoy our full inheritance in the future.

It is possible that, by the working of God's Spirit through such an approach, some people addicted to the theology of wealth might be jarred loose and have their values transformed into conformity with biblical values.

REORGANIZING THE STUDY OF A BIBLICAL PASSAGE

The same principles can be applied in the study of particular passages. We try to make new sense of the passage by looking at it from the viewpoint of a new theme or analogy. Taking a new view does not mean that we ignore or deny the internal themes of the passage. It means simply that we try to see whether we can notice something else about the passage by looking at it in a noncustomary way.

As an example, let us return one final time to Romans 7:14–25. Like any other passage, Romans 7 has an internal thematic organization and its own prominent themes. Because of the difficulty in interpreting this passage and the disputes over it, there is also some measure of disagreement over its internal themes. But it is not hard to see that the conflict over willing and doing good and evil is a major theme of verses 14–25. Moreover, the conflict is expressed in dramatic, almost psychologistic fashion. It is understandable that many people have adopted an interpretation along primarily psychological lines.

But suppose that, rather than using dramatic or psychologistic analogies as our main way of understanding the passage, we use as analogy any prominent theme within Paul's writings—for example, justification, union with Christ, or the hope for Christ's return. None of these starting points is guaranteed to reveal anything interesting. But in using one of them, we might turn up some connections that we would otherwise overlook. For instance, in looking at the passage in terms of union with Christ, we would naturally ask whether Paul is describing what he is in himself (apart from his union with Christ) in Romans 7:14–25 and what he is in Christ in chapter 8. Such a contrast still needs greater definition. But one can see that it is not necessarily quite the same as the contrast between regenerate and unregenerate and so might open the way to a new view.

In fact, not only Pauline themes but any prominent theme of the Bible can potentially be used as a perspective or window to look at Romans 7:14–25 in a new way. For the sake of illustration, let us use a rather unpromising theme: money. Once again, the theme must be expanded in order to be useful. If we expand it to include the whole complex concerning ownership, wealth, and exchange, we may begin to see at least some potential relevance to the passage. In verse 14, Paul specifically uses monetary language: he is "sold as a slave to sin." There is admittedly little other reference to money, but now we are only playing with a perspective or analogy to see whether it might throw light on the passage.

Let us go a step further. In Romans 7:23, Paul mentions "the members of my body." Paul is clearly the owner of his members. And yet, perversely and paradoxically, those members are apparently not under his control. We can construe this as a case of disputed ownership and disputed control. If Paul is "sold as a slave to sin," he is clearly owned by sin as master. He tries to assert his own ownership, by his desire for good, but finds that control is being exerted from other directions. It is still true that, from creation, he is owned by God.

Now we can already suggest one reason why Romans 7:14–25 is so hard to interpret. *Both* regenerate and unregenerate people experience some kind of contested ownership.

Unregenerate people are owned by sin and Satan. And yet they can never escape the fact that they are creatures, that they owe everything to God, and that God has power to dispose of them as He wills. On a psychological level God's ownership is acknowledged in the cries of guilty consciences. But the dispute between God and Satan is broader and deeper than just their consciences.

By contrast, regenerate people are owned by God and by righteousness. And yet, as long as they are in this life, sin and Satan still try to capture them and bring them under their ownership. The "flesh" still belongs to this realm (see, e.g., Gal. 5:16–18). This situation is manifested in psychological conflicts—but not only there.

Hence the presence of conflict does not by itself tell us who is being talked about in Romans 7:14–25. Moreover, it is clear that disputes about ownership exist on more than one level. On the one hand, there are legal facts to be established about who has the *right* of ownership. This issue is analogous to justification. On the other hand, there are facts about possession, that is, facts about current control over what one legally owns or does not own. The thief controls stolen goods but does not own them. The question of control (in particular, control over one's own actions) is analogous to sanctification.

On still another level, we can have a contrast between the situation of slavery under the Old Testament law and the situation of freedom since Christ has come (Gal. 4:1–7). In this sense even regenerate people in the Old Testament were owned by "the basic principles of the world" (v. 3). They were "bought" (redeemed) by Christ (v. 5). Hence conceivably the apparent contrast between Romans 7:14–25 and Romans 8 may be a contrast between pre-Pentecost slavery and post-Pentecost freedom (ownership of oneself).

What do we conclude from this analysis? We should retain our original judgment about prominent themes. Dramatic and psychological pictures, not ownership, are the primary vehicles of expression in Romans 7:14–25. But we may still have learned something. These dramatic and psychological pictures may be just that: pictures, vehicles of expression for realities that are not purely dramatic or psychological. Paul's primary purpose in using such language may be to impress on the reader the pathos and helplessness of the situation, not to produce an exact psychological theory. The realities to which he points include legal facts, ownership facts, facts about control, and facts characteristic of two kingdoms at war with each other. These facts are not exhausted by their psychic manifestations.

Our little exploration of money and ownership in Romans 7:14–25 has not solved all our problems. But it alerts us to the fact that there may be more than just two possible interpretations of this passage. When we are dealing with a difficult passage, anything that can move us away from a deadlock is worth looking at.

STUDYING THE THEMATIC RELATIONS OF BIBLICAL PASSAGES

One of the values of using a new analogy is that it may help us to relate one passage of the Bible to others. Sometimes the traditional way of interpreting a certain passage may so govern our thoughts that we do not notice potentially relevant parallels. Consider, for example, John 3:1–15, verses that have been widely taken as a classic passage about being "born again," about regeneration, about being saved by God after a previous life of sin and alienation from Him. The passage indeed is relevant to our understanding of regeneration. But does it say anything more? Let us see what happens with an altered disciplinary framework.

The traditional disciplinary framework for understanding John 3 is the framework of the theology of regeneration. But if we look at John 3 using the theme of fulfillment of the Old Testament or the theme of eschatology, we may notice what we did not notice before. In the Gospels a historical period of time is associated with "the kingdom of God" (vv. 3, 5). The phrase is not merely a designation for God's rule over the world from all eternity. Nor does it simply designate God's rule over human hearts. Rather, it is the exercise of God's rule in Christ's earthly life to save His people in a definite way. It is God's saving activity, to which the whole Old Testament looked forward. It is the fulfillment of Old Testament promises of God's salvation and the inauguration of the last days (i.e., eschatology in a broad sense).

Now in John 3, being "born anew" is closely related to being able to "see the kingdom of God." Being born anew may thus uniquely characterize the time of fulfillment. It is something that was prophesied would take place later, not something that occurred within the bounds of the Old Testament. Of course, regeneration, as systematic theology understands it, took place in the Old Testament. But John is discussing not regeneration as such but rather the fulfilled form that regeneration is to have now that Christ has come.

Jesus mentions the key role of the Spirit in being born anew (John 3:5–8). These comments agree with what he says to the Samaritan woman in John 4. Jesus himself provides the "living water," the water of the Spirit, and does so *after* his glorification (7:37–39; chap. 16). As Jesus says in 4:23, "A time is coming and has now come [*not* has always been] when the true worshipers will worship the Father in spirit and truth." In verse 21, he contrasts this time with the time when people worshiped at fixed locations (correctly at Jerusalem, incorrectly at Gerazim). When we link John 4 with John 16, we see that the Gospel of John must be talking about the depth of communion with God that is possible only after Pentecost.

Looking at John 3 from a new perspective has thus led us to a deeper and more accurate interpretation, primarily because it has enabled us to link it and other passages in John and elsewhere with the theme of fulfillment and eschatology. The chapter still has some implications for our doctrine of regeneration. But if we think that John 3 is directly discussing regeneration, with no focus on an eschatological coming of the Holy Spirit, we miss some of John's meaning.

As a second example, consider Psalm 23. All Christians are familiar with the practical use of this psalm with its meaning of the comfort, care, and protection of God. God undertakes to care for Christians just as He cared for Old Testament saints.

Many Christians have also gone a step further. They have

noted that, in John 10, Jesus calls himself the Good Shepherd. They also know the New Testament teaching concerning Christ's deity. When we put all these passages together, we see that Psalm 23 is a passage not only about the care of God the Father but about the care of Christ. Christ is our Shepherd and says to us the words of Psalm 23.

Thus we have a twofold use of this passage. It applies to the relation of God the Father to Christians, and to the relation of the Lord Jesus Christ to Christians. This twofold use has become something of a traditional disciplinary framework for the practical and devotional interpretation of Psalm 23.

I agree with this traditional twofold use. But I would suggest that something else is visible when we move outside the traditional disciplinary framework. We know that Christ is fully God. Hence it is legitimate to apply the words "the *Lord* is my shepherd" to Him. But what happens when we take a nontraditional look at the same words through the "window" of Christ's humanity?

The Psalms give inspired expression to the experience of the people of Israel in communion with God. Especially they are expressions related to the king of Israel, because the king was the representative of the people. Many of the psalms were in fact written by David or with David in view. David and godly descendants after him experienced the care of God their Shepherd.

Now the line of David's descendants led forward to Christ. Christ was the ultimate and climactic Son of David. As a human being, a descendant of David, He experienced the care of God during His earthly life. When He was confronted with difficulties and with enemies, He doubtless applied this psalm and others to Himself for sustenance. Psalm 23, for example, says that "even though I walk through the valley of the shadow of death, I will fear no evil" (v. 4). It speaks of rescue either from literal death or from a metaphorical analogy of death in the form of great distress, and life with God afterward (v. 6). Christ confronted not merely "the shadow of death" but real death. He was also rescued, not before He died but afterward, in His resurrection. And He now sits at God's right hand, having life with God forever. Because we are united with Christ in His life, death, resurrection, and rule, the psalm applies to us also.

Thus we see that Psalm 23 applies not only to the Father's relation to us and to Christ's relation to us but also to God the Father's relation to Christ. The use of a new perspective, outside of the traditional disciplinary framework, has alerted us to a new relationship between texts of the Bible.

Finally, let us consider David's fight with Goliath, narrated in 1 Samuel 17. Traditionally, Sunday schools have used the passage to give a moral lesson: Just as David had faith in God, stood up for God's name, and showed bravery for God's cause, so we should do today. Such a use expresses one valid perspective on the passage, since Old Testament passages are in many cases intended as examples for us (James 5:16–19; 1 Cor. 10:6–13).

Using a second perspective, we may note that the historical-critical tradition typically understands the passage as functioning to vindicate David's rise to kingship and to show that he is the man qualified by Yahweh to fill the role. This perspective also is valid.[2] In view of the interest of Samuel-Kings in the history of the kingship and in the contrast between Saul and David, we are invited to reflect on the politico-religious implications of this battle for Israel's understanding of its relation to the king chosen by God. Thus a perspective focusing on the corporate political implications of the passage within its immediate historical context is useful.

We may also use a perspective focusing on God and God's activity. We then note the faithfulness of God to David and God's power to turn events in the direction that He chooses, so that the outcome is contrary to human reckoning.

We may also use a perspective that asks about the role of mediators in the passage. When we ask that question, we realize that David, as the one anointed to become king, is a mediatorial

---

[2] In this case I agree with the *results* of the historical-critical tradition, not its presuppositions. Here, as elsewhere, I repudiate the antisupernaturalism and low view of Scripture inherent in the total framework.

representative of all the people in his combat. As the anointed one, he foreshadows Christ and Christ's kingship. Christ as the representative single-handedly triumphs over Satan in a decisive battle at the cross (Col. 2:15). David is thus emblematic of Christ's victory, and we enjoy the fruits of Christ's victory in a manner similar to the Israelite army's despoiling the Philistines (1 Sam. 17:51–53). Since the Old Testament kings and David in particular point forward to Christ (2 Sam. 7:13–14; Acts 13:22–23, 33–35), the parallel that we have drawn between David and Christ is not farfetched.

In sum, when we are studying a single passage like Psalm 23 or 1 Samuel 17, it is useful to adopt several different perspectives in order that we may notice several types of points being made and several types of possible connections with the message of the Bible as a whole. In particular, it is useful to ask (1) whether the human beings in a passage are analogous to us (e.g., David is an example for us of faith and bravery); (2) whether the passage reveals something of God's character that remains the same for us (e.g., God who is faithful to vindicate David will be faithful to us); (3) whether a mediatorial figure in a passage functions in a way illumining Christ's final mediatorship (e.g., David is a type of Christ); and (4) whether themes of a whole book of the Bible illumine the purpose of the passage (the theme of God's establishment of the kingly line and its destiny in 1 Samuel). In addition, we view the passage from the perspective of various prominent biblical themes: covenant, promise and fulfillment, judgment, temple, theophany, kingdom, eschatology, creation/re-creation, and so on.[3]

---

[3] The fourfold medieval allegorical approach to interpretation, though subject to excess, might be seen as a confused and poorly formulated attempt to see passages from a multiplicity of perspectives. In particular, we may ask whether passages are related to immediate propositional truth ("literal" meaning), to moral applications ("psychical" or "moral" meaning), to fulfillment in Christ and the church ("spiritual" meaning), or to the promise of the heavenly Jerusalem to which our history is progressing ("anagogical" meaning). In fact, many passages will to some degree manifest all four of these dimensions and other dimensions as well, when we see them in the context of the total canon of Scripture. The allegorical approach could not have survived as long as it did if it had not had a grain of truth.

12

PROSPECTS FOR DEEPENING OUR UNDERSTANDING OF THE BIBLE

The common thread through all our discussion has been the theme that world views, frameworks, and overall contexts influence knowledge and discovery in all areas. Knowledge is always qualified by its context. People know what they know against a background of other knowledge. This background includes both closely related knowledge in closely related fields and knowledge of a whole world view, some of which is tacit rather than known explicitly. In fact, all of us know many things that we do not realize that we know. If we are Americans, we know that we are supposed to knock at other people's front door to announce our presence. But in some cultures people cough instead of knocking. Such tacit knowledge is valuable, but it can also be dangerous. We can make assumptions that block out access to discovery (such as when we assume that everyone in other cultures has to knock at other people's doors).

Our background of knowledge colors any particular bit of knowledge and colors our expectations about what we will discover when we look at something new or when we look at something old for a second or third time. Because background knowledge is limited and differs from person to person, no one has a pristine neutral standpoint from which to acquire more knowledge. Such a situation is part of what it means to be a creature, to be finite. Hence it holds true for biblical interpretation and scientific investigation alike. Kuhn's work in the history and philosophy of science, by revising our idea of scientific method, makes more noticeable the parallels in this respect between science and biblical interpretation. Kuhn draws out attention to the contextualized character of knowledge in both fields.

The implications for biblical interpretation are multifarious. On the deepest level, we are challenged to become more aware of our dependence on God and of the significant role of the Holy Spirit and of our Christian commitment in influencing the acquisition of knowledge in general and biblical interpretation in particular (see chap. 9). Also, we become more aware of the contaminations of sin in the intellectual realm. We must train ourselves to detect alien, antibiblical presuppositions underlying the disciplinary frameworks for interpretation influenced by the Enlightenment. At the same time, none of us escapes the influence of our own sin or the sinful biases of the surrounding culture. Hence, we must be self-critical as well as critical of others.

Second, by becoming more aware of the influence of theological systems on interpretation, we are in a better position to conduct dialogue with those adhering to other systems.

Third, as the surrounding culture changes, we may be called upon to undertake a reorganization of our theological system or our interpretive practices in order, without compromising the biblical message, to communicate it more effectively to the people inhabiting the culture. Traditional Western theology has long been structured largely in terms of answering the question of guilt: How may I, a guilty sinner, escape condemnation before the holy and perfect Judge of the universe? But modern secularists find such questions less intelligible and less relevant than questions about the meaning of their life in a lonely, seemingly impersonal universe. A familial theology organized more prominently around the deeply personal categories of sonship and adoption may perhaps address secularists more effectively than a covenant theology organized more prominently around the question of legal guilt.

Both types of organization and both types of question are legitimate in principle, but one may be more useful as a point of contact.

Or again, in many Third World tribal cultures the prominent existential question is how to escape the power of evil spirits. Most of Western theology is far less equipped than is the Bible itself to address such a question.

Fourth, our observations about perspectives challenge us to look at old passages of the Bible in new ways. Sometimes a new perspective may open up for us new interpretive possibilities for difficult passages like Romans 7. Other times we will discover new truths about relatively uncontroversial passages like Psalm 23, or new relationships that passages like 1 Samuel 17 sustain to major themes of the Bible. In all this process, we will discover anew that the wisdom of God is unsearchably deep (Rom. 11:33–36).

APPENDIX

INTERPRETIVE METHOD AND OTHER FIELDS OF RESEARCH

In the course of our discussion we have here and there noticed points of contact between methods in biblical interpretation and methodological discussions in several different areas. I summarize here the points of contact with a larger body of literature, focusing particularly on the theme that larger contexts influence and qualify knowledge. Readers must remember that the people who write books and who have these ideas operate with their own presuppositions, which color what they know and what they write. We must therefore sift what is said in the light of our own presuppositions.

The Philosophy of Science

The philosophy of science has been vigorously discussing the contextual character of knowledge ever since the appearance of Thomas Kuhn's book. Various edited collections of articles interacting with Kuhn provide an introduction to the literature and the state of the discussion. One should note Gary Gutting, ed., *Paradigms and Revolutions* (Notre Dame: University of Notre Dame Press, 1980); Ian Hacking, ed., *Scientific Revolutions* (Oxford: Oxford University Press, 1981); Imre Lakatos and Alan Musgrave, eds., *Criticism and the Growth of Knowledge* (Cambridge: Cambridge University Press, 1970).

Predecessors of Kuhn also shared some of his interests in the contextual conditioning of scientific research. In his preface, Kuhn acknowledges the influence of Alexandre Koyré, *Etudes Galiléennes,* 3 vols. (Paris: Hermann, 1939); Emile Meyerson, *Identity and Reality* (New York: Macmillan, 1930); Hélène Metzger, *Les doctrines chimiques en France, du début du XVIIᵉ à la fin du XVIIIᵉ siècle* (Paris: Presses universitaires de France, 1923);

idem, *Newton, Stahl, Boerhaave et la doctrine chimique* (Paris: Alcan, 1930); and Anneliese Maier, *Die Vorläufer Galileis im 14. Jahrhundert* (Rome: Edizioni di storia e letteratura, 1949). See also Michael Polanyi, *Personal Knowledge: Towards a Post-Critical Philosophy* (Chicago: University of Chicago Press, 1958); idem, *Science, Faith, and Society* (Chicago: University of Chicago Press, 1964); idem, *The Tacit Dimension* (London: Routledge & Kegan Paul, 1967); Jean Piaget, *The Child's Conception of Physical Causality* (London: Routledge & Kegan Paul, 1930); idem, *Les notions de mouvement et de vitesse chez l'enfant* (Paris: Presses universitaires de France, 1946).

Other developments react in important ways to Kuhn. Some critics have simply misunderstood Kuhn, but there are also some significant positive developments. On the left of Kuhn, taking a more relativist, even anarchist, position, is Paul Feyerabend, *Against Method* (London: Verso, 1978). On the right of Kuhn, but endeavoring to take account of his insights, is Imre Lakatos, *The Methodology of Scientific Research Programmes* (Cambridge: Cambridge University Press, 1978). A significant extension of Kuhn in the direction of embedding scientific explanation in historical explanation is Alasdaire MacIntyre, "Epistemological Crises, Dramatic Narrative, and the Philosophy of Science," in *Paradigms and Revolutions,* ed. Gary Gutting (Notre Dame: University of Notre Dame Press, 1980), pp. 54–74.

Presuppositional Apologetics

Presuppositional apologetics as developed by Cornelius Van Til has emphasized the key role of presuppositions in theological and apologetic discussions. Presuppositions include not only consciously held philosophical assumptions but unconsciously assumed elements of one's world view. They are one's basic commitments.[1] Van Til has repeatedly emphasized the all-important question of religious roots, asking his reader in effect, Are you for God or against Him? Do you bow before God as

---

[1] See Frame, "God and Biblical Language."

your Lord, or do you wish to be your own god and lord? Do you endeavor to obey God, or do you obey your own autonomous ideas and standards? The antithesis between Christian and non-Christian life and thinking affects everything that we do. See Cornelius Van Til, *The Defense of the Faith*, 2d ed. (Philadelphia: Presbyterian & Reformed, 1963); idem, *An Introduction to Systematic Theology* (Phillipsburg, N.J.: Presbyterian & Reformed, 1974); idem, *A Christian Theory of Knowledge* (Philadelphia: Presbyterian and Reformed, 1969); idem, *Christian-Theistic Evidences* (Nutley, N.J.: Presbyterian and Reformed, 1976); Thom Notaro, *Van Til and the Use of Evidence* (Phillipsburg, N.J.: Presbyterian and Reformed, 1980); John M. Frame *The Doctrine of the Knowledge of God* (Phillipsburg, NJ: Presbyterian and Reformed, 1987). For an elementary introduction, see Richard L. Pratt, *Every Thought Captive: A Study Manual for the Defense of Christian Truth* (Phillipsburg, N.J.: Presbyterian and Reformed, 1979). Though some think that there are significant differences between Van Til and Francis Schaeffer, the latter's works also belong in this category. See especially Francis A. Schaeffer, *Escape from Reason* (Downers Grove, Ill.: InterVarsity, 1968); idem, *The God Who Is There* (Chicago: InterVarsity, 1968); idem, *He Is There and He Is Not Silent* (Wheaton, Ill.: Tyndale, 1972).

Ideas similar to Van Til's have also been articulated by the Christian philosophers in the tradition of cosmonomic philosophy. See Herman Dooyeweerd, *A New Critique of Theoretical Thought* (Philadelphia: Presbyterian and Reformed, 1969); Hendrik van Riessen, *Wijsbegeerte* (Kampen: Kok, 1970); Hendrik G. Stoker, *Beginsels en metodes in die wetenskap* (Potchefstroom: Pro Rege-Pers, 1961); Daniël F. M. Strauss, *Wysbegeerte en vakwetenskap* (Bloemfontein: Sacum, 1973). See also Nicholas Wolterstorff, *Reason Within the Bounds of Religion* (Grand Rapids: Eerdmans, 1976).

Van Til concentrated almost wholly on the question of religious basic commitments. The cultural outworkings of those commitments are less explored, although Francis Schaeffer and those associated with him have done important groundbreaking work in exploring the cultural effects. See, for example, Os Guinness, *The Dust of Death* (Downers Grove, Ill.: InterVarsity, 1973); Hendrik R. Rookmaaker, *Modern Art and the Death of a Culture* (London: InterVarsity, 1970). Moreover, the general idea that one needs to inspect the philosophical presuppositions of theological and scientific work has become fairly widespread in Evangelical circles. See, for example, John S. Feinberg, "Truth: Relationship of Theories of Truth to Hermeneutics"; Winfried Corduan, "Philosophical Presuppositions Affecting Biblical Hermeneutics"; and Millard J. Erickson, "Presuppositions of Non-Evangelical Hermeneutics"; all in *Hermeneutics, Inerrancy, and the Bible*, ed. Earl D. Radmacher and Robert D. Preus (Grand Rapids: Zondervan, 1984).

Relativistic Philosophy

Various forms of relativism and pragmatism have enjoyed a rapid growth of attention and interest because they focus on the relativity of pieces of knowledge to a whole framework or conceptual system. See, for example, the works of Nicholas Rescher, *Methodological Pragmatism* (New York: New York University Press, 1977); Richard Rorty, *Philosophy and the Mirror of Nature* (Princeton: Princeton University Press, 1979); Fredrick Christopher Swoyer, "Conceptual Relativism" (Ph.D. diss., University of Minnesota, 1976); Jack W. Meiland and Michael Krausz, eds., *Relativism, Cognitive and Moral* (Notre Dame: University of Notre Dame Press, 1982).

These philosophies may be called relativistic because they do not see any supposed knowledge as foundational. No area is immune to criticism for all time, no area is in principle so certain that we can say it is not subject to revision, no matter what may come. We may be confronted with facts or alternative interpretations that lead us to revise our world view. These philosophies, however, usually believe in truth of some kind, although they do not allow that we can achieve an absolute philosophical certainty about that truth. Hence they cannot be dismissed simply by using the typical antirelativist argument to the effect that, if all knowledge is relative, the statement "all knowledge is relative" is itself relative and therefore refuted.

Evangelical Christians, of course, know of a source of knowledge outside of the limitations of human finiteness. We can never adopt a full-fledged relativism. But we ought not for that reason to ignore the revival in relativistic philosophy. Non-Christians can still have insights about the implications of human finiteness.

Philosophical Hermeneutics

The phenomenological/existentialist tradition in philosophical hermeneutics has long been interested in the conditioned character of human understanding. In this tradition, human understanding always takes place against the background of assumptions and realities of human existence in history, existence as a person in society, existence as a person immersed in language as a pre- and supraindividual reality, and existence "unto death." The key figures are Heidegger and Gadamer. See Martin Heidegger, *Unterwegs zur Sprache* (Frankfurt am Main: Klostermann, 1985); Hans-Georg Gadamer, *Truth and Method* (New York: Seabury, 1975). One may also add the "hermeneutics of suspicion," practiced by people with interest in economic and political conditioning of ideologies and propaganda. See Jürgen Habermas, *Knowledge and Human Interests* (Boston: Beacon, 1972); idem, *Theorie und Praxis*, 3d ed. (Neuwied: Luchterhand, 1969). For a combined approach, see Paul Ricoeur, *Interpretation Theory* (Fort Worth: Texas Christian University Press, 1976); idem, *The Rule of Metaphor* (Toronto: University of Toronto Press, 1977).

Sociology of Knowledge

The sociology of knowledge has long dealt with ways in which the information and beliefs that a society counts as knowledge are passed along, maintained, legitimated, and supplemented by social processes and institutions. The sociology of knowledge makes clear the great dependence that knowledge has on a social setting for its maintenance. Kuhn's work might be understood as nothing more than the application of sociology of knowledge to the field of science. Sociology of knowledge is in fact interested in the social context for knowledge in any academic discipline, including biblical interpretation. It is also interested in the social context of the more informal and tacit knowledge of ordinary practitioners of religion. Many of the similarities that we have observed between biblical interpretation and Kuhn's view of science are similarities rooted in the general characteristics of the social context of all human knowledge.

Sociology of knowledge has roots even in the previous century, but it received a kind of formal inauguration with Karl Mannheim, *Ideology and Utopia: An Introduction to the Sociology of Knowledge* (New York: Harcourt, Brace & World, 1968; orig. ed., 1929). One may find more up-to-date discussion in Peter L. Berger and Thomas Luckmann, *The Social Construction of Reality: A Treatise in the Sociology of Knowledge* (Garden City, N.Y.: Doubleday, 1966); Irving L. Horowitz, *Philosophy, Science, and the Sociology of Knowledge* (Westport, Conn.: Greenwood, 1976); Michael Mulkay, *Science and the Sociology of Knowledge* (London: Allen & Unwin, 1979); K. J. Regelous, ed., *The Sociology of Knowledge* (New York: State Mutual, 1980); Gunter W. Remmling, ed., *Towards the Sociology of Knowledge: Origin and Development of a Sociological Thought Style* (Atlantic Highlands, N.J.: Humanities, 1974); Nico Stehr and Volker Meja, eds., *Society and Knowledge: Contemporary Perspectives on the Sociology of Knowledge* (New Brunswick, N.J.: Transaction, 1984); Susan J. Hekman, *Hermeneutics and the Sociology of Knowledge* (Notre Dame: Notre Dame University Press, 1983).

Anthropology

The field of cultural anthropology includes numerous studies of the influence of world views and the influence of culture on knowledge. Here I refer readers only to Evangelical discussions of the implications of anthropology. See especially Harvie M. Conn, *Eternal Word and Changing Worlds: Theology,*

Anthropology, and Mission in Trialogue (Grand Rapids: Zonder-
van, 1984); Paul G. Hiebert, *Cultural Anthropology*, 2d ed.
(Grand Rapids: Baker, 1983); Charles H. Kraft, *Christianity in
Culture: A Study in Dynamic Biblical Theologizing in Cross-
Cultural Perspective* (Maryknoll, N.Y.: Orbis, 1979).

Theological Method

Some discussions are also taking place concerning the
implications of contexts for our methods of biblical interpretation. Liberation theology and contextualization (as the term is
used in missions theory) both study the influence of culture on
the shape of our theological questions and answers. They
involve strenuous reexamination of traditional interpretive
method. The radicals in these areas are advocating something
like a Kuhnian revolution in method.[2]

More to the point are discussions of the implications of
modern science for biblical interpretation. As we noted at the
beginning of this book, many discussions have considered the
relation of science and theology. But there have been fewer
discussions on scientific *method* in comparison with theological
method.[3] Still less has recent work taken into account Kuhn's

---

[2] See volume 7 in the series Foundations of Contemporary Interpretation
(Grand Rapids: Zondervan, forthcoming).

[3] Despite expressed concerns for theological method, Thomas F. Torrance's
work should be classified with others that explore the general topic of science
and theology. His procedure is more like that of a philosopher building a world
view or an epistemology than it is like Kuhn's sociological approach. See
Torrance's works, *Christian Theology and Scientific Culture* (New York: Oxford
University Press, 1981), *Divine and Contingent Order* (Oxford: Oxford University Press, 1981), *Reality and Evangelical Theology* (Philadelphia: Westminster,
1982), and *Transformation and Convergence in the Frame of Knowledge* (Grand
Rapids: Eerdmans, 1984). In *Transformation and Convergence*, Torrance mentions
Kuhn (p. 243) and notes the conditioning character of world views and the
social backgrounds of knowledge, especially the philosophical dualisms of
modern Western thought (e.g., pp. x–xiii). Nevertheless, Kuhn has not
substantially influenced Torrance. A closer analysis shows that Torrance selects
from modern physics and from philosophical epistemology just those features
that he finds convenient for analogically illustrating his Barthian theology. His
presuppositions greatly influence what he selects and how he describes it.

move away from the idea that science presents us with a purely objective, disinterested account of the way the world is. The most notable exception is Ian G. Barbour, *Myths, Models, and Pardigms: A Comparative Study in Science and Religion* (New York: Harper & Row, 1974).[4] Barbour's book is a very important work in this area because it stands almost alone in being a post-Kuhnian attempt to spell out some of the connections between science and religion on a methodological level.

But Barbour's book does not do all that one might wish. In the first place, Barbour is interested mostly in the comparison of science and *religion,* not science and Christianity or science and theology. He is most concerned with philosophical issues concerning the viability of religious language in general. On this philosophical level, Barbour's book contains many useful ideas. But he says too little about the implications for hermeneutical method and the academic subdisciplines of biblical interpretation. What he does say shows that he is uncomfortable with the exclusive claims of Christianity, the claims of propositional revelation, and the orthodox doctrine of God.[5] In particular, when Barbour provides us with examples of alternative models for Christ and for God, the newer alternatives are heterodox. Though Barbour is interested in world views, he is not willing to challenge in a radical way the dominant Western dream of human autonomy in thought. Hence Evangelicals will find here a mixture of good and bad. If we wish to find a book that reforms biblical interpretation on the basis of a biblical world view, we will have to look elsewhere.

Torrance's work is thus more an illustration of Kuhn's observations about the role of frameworks and presuppositions than a continuation or supplement to Kuhn's work.

[4]Note also a related book by Barbour, *Issues in Science and Relgion* (New York: Harper & Row, 1971). Some very sweeping appeals to paradigm shifts appear in James P. Martin, "Toward a Post-Critical Paradigm," *New Testament Studies* 33 (1987): 370–85.

[5]Barbour, *Myths, Models, and Paradigms,* pp. 8, 176–77; pp. 18, 134, 138; idem, *Issues in Science and Religion.*

My own book *Symphonic Theology: The Validity of Multiple Perspectives in Theology* (Grand Rapids: Zondervan, 1987) works out the methodological problems related to the practice of single-perspective versus multiple-perspective approaches to theological problems. Many of its concerns are similar to those I discuss in this book. But *Symphonic Theology* interacts primarily not with Kuhn but with internal developments within theology and linguistics and should be seen as complementary to the discussions in this book.

INDEX OF AUTHORS AND TITLES

INDEX OF SUBJECTS
AND PERSONS

INDEX OF BIBLICAL PASSAGES